PREACHING THE SCRIPTURES

DEDICATION

This book is dedicated to all African heroes and heroines of the faith who risked all for Christ; and to all African preachers who seek to preach nothing but the Scripture – the whole of it and the truth of it.

PREACHING THE SCRIPTURES

Joel Kamsen Tihitshak Biwul

HIPPOBOOKS

ACTS

AFRICA
CHRISTIAN
TEXTBOOKS

Langham

CREATIVE PROJECTS

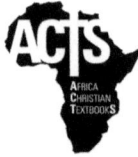

CONTENTS

FOREWORD

I was honoured when Dr. Joel Biwul asked me to write the foreword to his book. When the manuscript arrived, I was in the middle of preparing lessons for my class the next day. I said, "Well, let me simply read a couple of sentences. I will read the rest of the manuscript tomorrow." So I read the first couple of sentences. But then I carried on reading. I did not want to put the book down. Before I knew it, I had finished the chapter.

In *Preaching the Scriptures* Dr. Joel Biwul addresses fundamental issues in ministry profoundly yet simply. His message grips you, and so does the way he communicates it. His stories and illustrations help drive the message home as he looks at the challenges in preaching and takes you through the process of preparing and delivering a sermon. His examples are clear and helpful.

In Africa, as everywhere, the church badly needs preachers who preach the Scriptures to bring people to Christ and nurture them in the faith. Many preachers are preaching themselves and their own interests. Many are preaching in ignorance of the Scriptures. Therefore, Dr. Biwul's book is timely. He stresses the awesome honour and privilege of being a preacher of God's word – a spokesman for God from the pulpit. You would not want, as Dr. Biwul puts it, to be a channel that feeds error into God's church. I therefore highly recommend this book to every pastor and indeed to all Christians. I pray that God will use *Preaching the Scriptures* mightily in his church.

Rt. Rev. Dr. Michael Kyomya
Jinja, Uganda
10 April 2017

ACKNOWLEDGEMENTS

Although every author claims responsibility for what he or she writes, no reasonable book is exclusively the author's independent product without the contributions of a number of other people. This book is no exception.

I am very deeply thankful to Bishop Michael Kyomya, who graciously agreed to write the foreword for this book. I would also like to express my deep gratitude to HippoBooks for agreeing to publish it, and to my editors, Dahlia Fraser and Isobel Stevenson, who contributed to making this book what it is. As editors they are firm and detail-oriented when it comes to professional quality, yet also friendly and sacrificial. Isobel's friendship and kindness have been an immense blessing in every sense of the word. I must also thank her husband for giving her the support she needs as she supports others.

Various reviewers who read my proposal and my manuscripts have also contributed to the shaping of this book. In particular, I would like to thank Martin Goodchild and his wife Susie for their willingness to act as sounding boards. It was a privilege to work with them, and their comments and suggestions have helped make this book a reality.

The critical comments and useful suggestions of my preliminary editor Hauwa John-Ramadan were also much appreciated. She guided my tone and writing style and made me think more critically and carefully than I had done. Thank you Hauwa!

At almost all of our family devotions, my wife and children would pray for my many writing projects – whether articles or books. This book is a result of their prayers. I remain ever grateful for having such a lovely family.

Finally, I would like to thank my students at ECWA Theological Seminary (JETS), Jos, Nigeria who urged me to write a book on preaching each time I taught the course in homiletics. Here is the book you were asking for!

Thank you all of you.

1

INTRODUCTION

There are many good Christian speakers in Africa, but not many good preachers.

Let me explain what I mean. "Good Christian speakers" are people who can talk about the Bible, perhaps even talk about it very well. They can quote a lot of verses. But that does not necessarily make them good preachers. What makes a good preacher is the ability not just to quote the Bible but also to explain what it means. A good preacher shows how the passage being preached on applies to those who are listening to the preacher. They learn how to put what they hear to good use.

I can illustrate the difference between a good speaker and a good preacher from Scripture itself. In Acts 8:26–35 we read about an encounter between Philip and an Ethiopian official. The official was an educated and godly man who had made a long journey from North Africa to Jerusalem to worship in the temple. He could probably speak very well – then, as now, that ability was a requirement for anyone in an important position. If you had asked him why he was going to Jerusalem, he could have told you the reasons and he could have quoted from the Bible to back them up. When Philip met him, he was reading from the book of Isaiah. But when Philip asked him, "Do you understand what you are reading?" He replied, "How can I, unless someone explains it to me?" Philip then became a good preacher, explaining what the passage he was reading meant, not only in general terms but also in terms of how it applied to the official himself.

Like that Ethiopian man many zealous, religious people read the Bible but struggle to understand it. They have a general idea of its teaching on morality because that is often in keeping with traditional African values.

But they do not have any deep understanding of how the teachings of the Bible can directly affect their spiritual lives and their everyday lives as fathers, mothers, employees, employers, students, teachers, business persons, consumers, neighbours, leaders, voters and politicians.

We see the effects of that lack of knowledge in the many ills that afflict our continent. We see it when people try to redefine who Jesus is by dressing him in the clothes of African Traditional Religion. We see it in the way people flock to those who use religion as a means to gain wealth and power. Too often church members fall prey to these preacher predators.

How are Christians to learn to understand the Scriptures better? The answer is that they need good preachers to help them. Those preachers need to be prepared and capable Christians who know God, understand the Bible, and are able to preach clearly. Such preachers can show the relevance of the Bible to daily life in Africa. But more than that, such preachers can help Africans understand who God is, what he has done for them and will do for them, and what it means to be a mature Christian.

There are, of course, already many preachers in Africa. But some of them are false shepherds who preach only to extort money from their hearers. Some are careless, and do not realize the importance of their work as preachers. Some are lazy and not prepared to do the hard work needed to preach well. All they want is to hear the sound of their own voices expressing their own opinions. This book is not for such preachers.

However, there are other preachers who know that the Bible is the word of God. They long to preach all of it faithfully. They want to see people grow to maturity in their faith. But they know that they are not succeeding in doing this. They worry about how to preach and what to preach. This book is intended to help all such preachers learn the art of preaching from the Scriptures. Its goal is to help untrained lay preachers or evangelists correctly handle the word of truth.

In this book you will learn more about the need for what is called expository preaching and will find simple tools that you can use to feed others with the bread of life. It shows how preachers can use all of Scripture for "teaching, rebuking, correcting and training in righteousness" (2 Tim 3:16) so that all God's people in Africa are equipped to serve him faithfully.

But before we explore what good preaching is, we need to identify some harmful forms of preaching that are very common in Africa. That is why the next chapter is titled "What Preaching is Not".

2

WHAT PREACHING IS NOT

I once walked into a local restaurant feeling very hungry. As I placed my order, the waiter informed me that their policy was "pay before service". So I paid in advance for the food. But when the food arrived, I could not eat it. It was sour, watery, and had far too much pepper. Not wanting to complain and attract attention, I quietly walked out of the restaurant. I would never go there again.

Just as this bad food could not satisfy my hunger, so bad preaching and wrong use of the Bible cannot meet the spiritual needs of church members. When preaching is not done rightly, the listeners leave hungry and dissatisfied. Some may never return to that church, or to any church.

But there are also other types of bad food, where the problem is not apparent at first glance. Think of what we call "junk food". It looks attractive, others speak highly of it, and we sometimes enjoy eating it. But those who eat only junk food will find that their health begins to suffer because it lacks nutritional value. Similarly, those who hear "junk preaching" may enjoy it at first, but will eventually find that they are suffering from spiritual malnutrition.

How can we tell the difference between nutritious preaching and junk preaching? One way to do this is to ask whether what the preacher says and does in the pulpit focuses our attention on God and his word or diverts our attention from God.

Preaching Is Not Self-Advertisement

Some preachers divert our attention from God by using the pulpit and preaching as a way to advertise themselves. "They give themselves titles like "Anointed Man of God" and "President and Founder", and want to be called "Papa" and "Mama". They boast about the number of degrees they have acquired and the types of cars they own. When they preach, they talk about what God has used them to do and what he can do through them or their ministry. They announce that those who come to their church will receive miracles of healing, gain material wealth, and be protected from their enemies and from what they call "untimely death".

But true preaching is not talking about oneself. True preaching is telling people about Christ and his kingdom. He is at the centre of Christian preaching. True preachers recognize that they are only the instruments through which Christ is preached. Even the great Apostle Paul described himself as only "a servant of Christ" (Rom 1:1; Phil 1:1; Titus 1:1) or "an apostle of Christ Jesus" (1 Cor 1:1; 2 Cor 1:1; Gal 1:1; Eph 1:1; Col 1:1; 1 Tim 1:1; 2 Tim 1:1). He was determined that all his preaching would be about "Jesus Christ and him crucified" (1 Cor 2:1–5).

Like Paul, true preachers recognize that it is a great privilege to preach God's word. They acknowledge that they are not worthy of this honour and that it is only by God's grace that they are allowed to preach at all. So they preach with an attitude of humility and in full submission to the Lordship of Christ. They are mindful that all that they say and do reflects on him, and they seek to honour him in how they live. So they preach about Christ and do not seek to draw attention to themselves.

Preaching Is Not Telling Endless Stories

Many Africans are superb storytellers. And we all enjoy hearing a well-told story. When we were children, we learnt by listening to the stories our parents or the village elders told us. So a wise preacher will use stories in preaching, just as Jesus did. (You will see that I have even used some stories in this book.)

However, there are some preachers who get carried away when telling stories. Instead of explaining what the Bible says, they use the sermon as an opportunity to demonstrate their storytelling skills. They tell aimless, endless stories, of the kind Nigerians call "tales by moonlight".

Sometimes these stories overlap with the self-advertisement I referred to above. This happens when preachers tell stories about themselves to impress their listeners. They talk about the countries they have visited, the politicians and businesspeople they know, the social status of their friends, the delicious food they have eaten and the type of fruit juice they like to drink.

When stories replace preaching, the sermon becomes a form of entertainment with the preacher as storyteller. Going to church becomes like attending a social gathering; it is a place where you can relax and have fun. Christians who are not seriously committed to the faith, and even non-Christians, will attend church in order to be entertained and to get some good stories that they can retell during the week. They will laugh at all the preacher's jokes, no matter how unnecessary or even distasteful. They really like the flavour of this "junk food".

But the preacher of God's word should not be a storyteller, a clown or a joker. Preachers have been given the great honour of representing God in the pulpit, and what they should be doing is preaching the word of God. To do otherwise is to abuse their privilege and to deny God the glory and honour due to him. That was why the Apostle Paul advised preachers that they should not preach the gospel "with words of human wisdom, lest the cross of Christ be emptied of its power" (1 Cor 1:17). True worshippers do not come to church to be entertained but to hear God speak to them.

Preaching Is Not Using the Bible as a Charm

In Africa there is a strong belief in magical powers, witchcraft, and the ability of evil spirits to harm people. As a result, many preachers encourage their listeners to see the Bible as a charm they can use for protection against these forces. This way of using the Bible is bolstered in some parts of Africa by the influence of Islam, for some Muslims use the Qur'an in a similar way. They write out certain portions of the

Qur'an and wear them as amulets, or copy verses from the Qur'an onto a tablet of some kind, which they then carefully wash so that the ink dissolves in the water. They believe that drinking water with holy words dissolved in it confers special benefits.

Some Christian preachers encourage believers to do the same with the Bible. They let them treat it as a magic book. For example, Christians are told to sleep with a Bible under their pillow. Or they are instructed to recite certain portions of the Bible before retiring to bed at night or before embarking on a journey. The aim is not to increase their understanding of the Bible or develop their faith but rather to secure God's protection from witches, wizards, evil spirits and accidents. This kind of preaching does not draw people to God and to his word. When the Bible is used as a charm or as a book with magical powers, it becomes an idol. We are honouring the book rather than the God who gave it to us.

Preaching Is Not Using the Bible as a Whip

Some preachers in Africa avoid the trap of treating the Bible as a magic charm, but instead they choose to use it as a whip. They are like the pastor talking about his latest sermon who told a friend, "I really gave it to them!" Such preachers quote the Bible to chastise and control church members. They like to preach on portions of the Bible like Psalm 105:15: "Do not touch my anointed ones; do my prophets no harm." But they do not look at these verses in context; they simply use them to boost their own power and to protect their own position and interests. They use their time in the pulpit to demand respect from church members or parishioners and from the church board or council. To them, "respect" means that no one is allowed to hold them accountable or ask them to explain their actions.

Now, there is much truth in the African proverb, "You can never greet all the people in the market." We cannot please everybody. There are some church members who do act like enemies. They oppose whatever the pastor or priest does and says. In such a situation, a pastor can be tempted to use the privilege of preaching to get back at hostile members. But preaching is not meant to be a threat. Preaching that instils dread enslaves the listener. It has a negative effect on the quality of Christian spirituality. Rather than preaching "at" rebellious members we should preach "to" them. The right use of the Bible in preaching will help, heal, encourage and give hope to the listeners. We should gently and lovingly confront sinners to bring them to faith, not scare them or make them more hardened.

Real Food or Junk Food?

I well remember the wise words of one of my church members: "Pastor, we members know you pastors. We talk about you when we meet in the places where we relax. We know which pastor is a beggar and which one is not; we know who plays politics and who serves their church. We know which pastor can preach the Bible well and which one cannot; and we also know which pastor tells us the truth and which one does not."

In the long run, our hearers are not fooled. They can recognise when a preacher forfeits the respect, integrity, and dignity that should go with being the mouthpiece of God. This ought to challenge us to preach God's word correctly and adequately. We should never send those who listen to us home empty, with their ears filled only with "tales by moonlight".

Above all, God is not fooled. He knows whether we have been faithful servants, faithfully communicating his message, rather than our own message. He knows whether our words have directed people to him and to his word. He knows whether our preaching has made the Bible come alive and become more meaningful to our hearers, or whether all that they hear is our own story.

3

WHAT BIBLICAL PREACHING IS

Centuries ago, God used a zealous converted Jew as his instrument to carry the gospel from town to town. The man's name was Paul. As he travelled around preaching, he came to a town called Ephesus, where some young men, whom the Bible calls the "seven sons of Sceva", tried to imitate him by using the name of Jesus to heal a demon-possessed man. The outcome was not good. The evil spirit cried out, "Jesus I know, and I know about Paul, but who are you?" and then the possessed man pounced on them and they had to run for their lives (Acts 19:11–16).

Today there are many African preachers who are like the seven sons of Sceva in that they just copy what they see other preachers do or repeat what they have heard others say. They do not know what biblical preaching actually involves, or how to do it effectively. So in this chapter, we will look at what biblical preaching is. Does it involve more than just mentioning the Bible somewhere in a sermon?

Biblical Preaching Is About Christ

Earlier, I said that preaching is not self-advertisement. It should never be used to advertise yourself. Instead, biblical preaching should advertise God. Christian preaching is all about God and his glory. It speaks of Christ and his kingdom. It flows out of the preacher's deep personal convictions about God and his word, not from any concern for the preacher's personal interests.

Jesus Christ must always be the core or centre of every sermon. In saying this, I am not saying that every passage in the Bible has to be forced to be explicitly or symbolically about Christ. Rather, I am saying that the heart of Christian preaching is always about telling people what God has done for us in Jesus Christ. It is telling people about God's love for them and what he expects them to do. In preaching we are not merely reporting an event recorded in the Bible or teaching about good behaviour; we are declaring, proclaiming and communicating, from personal conviction, the message of the Bible to the hearer. That is what Christian preaching is.

Since biblical preaching has Christ at its centre, true Christian preaching can be done only by people whose lives have been transformed through the death and resurrection of Jesus Christ.

Biblical Preaching Is Based on the Bible

Preachers whose lives have truly been transformed by Christ do not waste time telling endless stories or "tales by moonlight". They may use stories, as Christ did, but the stories do not dominate their message. They know that all their preaching must point to Christ. They also know that the Bible is the ultimate source that points to Christ, for it contains both his teachings and teaching about him. Such preachers understand the value of God's word, respect it, and work hard to use it rightly when preaching. It is where they find their message, and it is the authority they use to back up what they say.

In the class I teach on the principles of biblical preaching, I always remind my students that when preaching, they must "deal with the text, stay with the text, and stay in the text". In other words, they need to remember that true Christian preaching is always Bible-centred. It must explain the meaning of the Bible without wandering away from it, and it must present the message of the Bible to people.

Biblical Preaching Delivers a Message from God

Preachers who use the Bible as a charm are only interested in its power, not in its message. But biblical preachers are eager to deliver that message. They do not want to speak for themselves, but for the one who has sent them.

Think of what happens when the president of a country sends his representative to deliver a policy speech at an important gathering like the United Nations or the African Union. The diplomat does not have the authority to alter the message that was prepared for the occasion. He must say exactly what is in the speech, no more and no less. And he must take his responsibility very seriously. If he gets something wrong, it will reflect badly on the president who sent him.

In a similar manner, a preacher setting out to preach the Bible needs to approach the matter with all the seriousness it deserves. Our position is similar to that of John the Baptist, who came to announce that Jesus was coming (Matt 3:1–15; John 1:15, 19–27), or like that of the Old Testament prophets. They saw themselves as the messengers of God, acting as his mouthpiece to deliver his word to the people. That is why they often began their messages by saying, "This is what the LORD says". As the Lord's messengers, they did not add to or subtract from the message they were given. They spoke exactly what God told them without compromise or negotiation and without playing politics with the message.

We as preachers have been given God's written word, the Bible, and it is now our responsibility to present God's word to the people. This means that there is a sense in which we too represent God when we stand before people in the pulpit. That is an awesome responsibility that we should never take lightly! It means that we are not at liberty to do what we please with God's word when we preach. It must guide all that we say. We must be loyal and obedient servants, obeying what God says in the Bible.

Biblical Preaching Transforms Lives

Preachers who use the Bible as a whip are trying to transform lives. But they are going about it the wrong way, and sometimes with the wrong motives. We cannot scold people into the kingdom of God. Nor can we transform lives simply by saying the same thing over and over again. Only God can change people and their situations. So when we preach, our task is to proclaim what God has said, and then ask God to apply these truths to our hearers in a way that does in fact transform their lives.

When I was serving as a pastor, I had a practice that reminded me of this truth. Every Saturday evening after all the various church groups had finished their programmes, I would go into the sanctuary to pray in preparation for Sunday. I would kneel by the pulpit and ask God for special anointing upon me for the following day as I represented him in the pulpit through preaching. Then I would kneel by every row of benches and ask that God would bless all those who would be sitting on them. I was asking him to do the work of transforming their lives.

God honours such prayer. If you pray like this, you can present the Scriptures with confidence, expecting to see spiritual changes in people; changes in their struggles with the challenges of poverty; changes in their relationships with their family, friends, and neighbours; changes in the way they respond to temptations and the frustrations of life.

Biblical Preaching Is a Serious Task

Why do you preach? Why will you continue to preach? Is it just because it is what a pastor does? Or is it just because you enjoy sharing your opinions with others, without them interrupting you? What would be your honest answer to the question of why you preach?

It amazes me that some African Christian preachers take the task of preaching lightly and even carelessly. They think it is easy and do not bother to spend much time preparing to preach. For me, preaching is the most difficult task I have ever undertaken.

Why is it so difficult? It is because it imposes so many responsibilities. For one thing, I need to make sure that I am proclaiming God's word accurately. So I need to study it carefully to make sure I am doing this. We will talk more of this later.

Then, because the message is so important, and because I know that I am a very inadequate representative of God, I have to invest time in self-preparation. I have learnt from experience that I need to make every effort to find time to fast and pray for every sermon that I preach.

But these are not my only responsibilities. I also have a responsibility to meet the needs of the people to whom I preach every Sunday. So I need to know what their lives are like. What events and issues are affecting them? I must be their friend who shares their pain; their counsellor when they face discomfort, pain and frustration. I must try to help them find answers to the many questions they have about God and about their lives. All of these factors will affect me as I try to decide what to preach and how to preach it in a way that will meet their needs. This too is a great challenge.

Moreover, as preachers, we must pay attention not only to the material needs of our church members but also to the spiritual condition of all who listen to our preaching. We know that people are fallen and stand in need of grace. Even those who are saved need grace for their daily lives. The destiny of human souls should weigh on us whenever we stand up to preach. It could be that your sermon will be the last opportunity someone has to hear God speak and come to faith or be restored in their relationship with God.

As preachers, the awesome responsibility of balancing, in the same sermon, God's expectation of the listeners and the listeners' expectations from God should drive us to our knees. It should also drive us to learn as much as we can about preaching so that we are better equipped to do this task.

4

WHY BIBLICAL PREACHING IS NEEDED

So far, I have been talking about what preaching is and is not. But there is still one very important question that has not been answered – why is biblical preaching needed? Churches across Africa are full. Preachers are already preaching every Sunday. So why be concerned about a lack of biblical preaching?

African Christian Spirituality Needs Revival

When the Western missionaries came with the gospel to Africa, our ancestors accepted the message. Many communities relinquished African Traditional Religion with all its beliefs and practices.

The first generation of African Christians treasured the new religion. They not only enthusiastically accepted the gospel, they also practised it with zeal. They were willing to die for their new faith in Jesus. Some of the early leaders of independent African countries such as Kenneth Kaunda of Zambia and Nnamdi Azikiwe of Nigeria were greatly influenced by the power of Christianity in Africa.

But something went wrong. The zeal and commitment of those early converts is not seen in their successors. If the early African converts to Christianity were to come back, they would weep and refuse to be comforted at the sight of Christian spirituality in modern Africa.

Why is this? One reason is that many who claim to be Christian today are merely Christian in name, not in lifestyle. The Apostle Paul describes such Christians as holding to the form of Christianity while their lives deny the power of the gospel (2 Tim 3:5). They may call themselves Christians, but they do not live like Christians.

Sadly, this is true even of some who are now church leaders. A number of them are more concerned about earthly pleasures than about eternal and spiritual things. They do not obey John's warning not to love the world or the things in it (1 John 2:15–17). They themselves need spiritual revival if they are to be able to preach Christ. They are like the religious leaders of Jesus' day (the Pharisees) whom Jesus described as blind guides. He said of them, "If a blind man leads a blind man, both will fall into a pit" (Matt 15:14).

Tribal sentiments have also found their way into the church. The strong ties that should bind Christians from all parts of the continent together are being eroded by an emphasis on people's tribal identity. Sometimes people are considered for church leadership positions on the basis of what tribe they belong to. Worse, in some churches, pastors or priests are considered for ordination for ministry on the basis of their tribal affiliation.

There is thus a need to revive biblical Christianity in modern Africa through proper biblical preaching done with zeal, commitment, passion, and the dedication that it deserves. African preachers must call Christians back to the "old time religion" by faithfully preaching the truth of the Bible. As the old hymn says:

> Revive us again,
> Fill each heart with thy love;
> May each soul be rekindled
> With fire from above.

African Moral Values Need Revival

Africans have a long moral tradition that involved the whole community. People lived together and cared for one another in the community. They engaged in communal labour and the whole community was involved in training the young. There was an emphasis on co-operation, support and mutual responsibility.[1]

This African understanding of morality and its practice is similar to what we find in the Bible. For instance, in the Bible children are told to respect their parents (Exod 20:12; Deut 5:16; Matt 15:4; Eph 6:2); people are told to love and care for their neighbours (Lev 18:19; Matt 19:19; Rom 12:9–10); they are told not to steal and not to be sexually immoral (Deut 27:20; Lev 18:7–16, 20; 20:11, 19–21); members of a community are required to show hospitality to visitors (Deut 10:19; Rom 12:13; 1 Pet 4:9; Heb 13:2); people in every community are to live by practising and protecting truth, fairness and justice (Lev 19:13, 15; Deut 5:20); and so on.

Among the negative changes taking place in Africa today is the gradual disappearance of some of these cherished moral values. We are forgetting about respect for the elderly, obedience to our parents, caring for our neighbour's property and welfare, and working together rather than going our separate ways. These values have been replaced by a culture that tolerates theft, armed robbery, dishonesty, laziness, immorality, and many other bad behaviours. We see children who no longer value and care for their parents. The children live in the city and never take time to visit their parents in the village or provide for their needs. Some people no longer respect the elderly and offer to help them carry goods along the road. Even the culture of greeting people we meet along the way is dying, although we expect to be greeted ourselves. These negative behaviours are not likely to be changed by African politicians or rehabilitation centres. The antidote that is needed is a simple but clear presentation of the Scriptures.

This is where the role of the African preacher comes in. In his book, *African Religions and Philosophy*,[2] John Samuel Mbiti describes African people as deeply religious and living in a densely religious universe or environment. Because they value spiritual things, Africans will usually respect and obey the instructions of their spiritual leaders. So as spiritual leaders, preachers should make a conscious effort to use clear biblical

---

[1] Samuel Waje Kunhiyop deals with this in more detail in *African Christian Ethics* (Jos/Nairobi: Hippo, 2008).

[2] London: Heinemann, 1969; revised 1990.

preaching to educate their listeners on biblical principles so that they can apply them to their day-to-day lives.

African Traditional Religion Is Being Revived

We are currently witnessing a revival of African Traditional Religion in some parts of the continent. Even some Christians are turning to ancestral spirits in an attempt to gain power and be protected from their enemies. Why are people who have inherited a good spiritual legacy returning to traditional religion in an enlightened generation? What is making African Traditional Religion attractive to such Christians today?

There is a saying, "Water cannot taste sour without a reason." One of the reasons people, and particularly young people, are returning to traditional religions is the rise in insurgencies, tribal strife, communal clashes, and wars. People are scared, and will turn to any power that offers protection, including the religious practices of their ancestors. They do this because the message of the Bible has not been clearly presented to them in a way that is understandable and meaningful. So they have not been able to develop deep spiritual roots. Much of what they hear preachers say in sermons seems to be superficial and repetitive. Usually, the listeners are simply told what the Bible says, which some of them can read for themselves, but they are not taught how to apply the Bible's teaching in practical ways in their own lives. They are left with many unanswered questions.

Not only is the Bible poorly presented, but to many people the God of Christianity seems too slow to act. People don't like to wait for anything, especially in this twenty-first century when everyone seems to be in a hurry. In the words of Nigerian street English, people want things done "sharp, sharp". The Christian God seems slow, while the gods and spirits of traditional religion seem to act faster in response to people's urgent needs. Just as in the West, people go for fast food to save time; so in Africa people seek quick solutions to their problems. In fact, there is a church in Jos, Nigeria, called The God of Now, Now. Many Christians flock to this church because they want God's solution to their needs "now, now". The same sense of urgency drives some Christians to turn to witchcraft and the occult, consulting fortune-tellers, mediums, medicine men, spiritualists, and the spirits of the ancestors. Those who are too religious to use these means seek prophecies from fake prophets.

In the 1970s, Byang H. Kato, the first leader of the Association of Evangelicals in Africa, pointed out the likelihood of Christianity in Africa reverting to traditional religion in the near future. He warned of a growing syncretism in which people would try to worship the God of Christianity and the gods of African Traditional Religion at the same time. He also spoke out against the belief in universal salvation, which holds that all belief systems are equal since "all roads lead to heaven".

Today we are experiencing what Kato foresaw. This reversion poses a great danger to the gospel and to the Christian life and testimony in Africa. It should thus attract the attention of African preachers. Their preaching of the gospel and of the message of the cross has to be clear, correct, appropriate, relevant, and completely Bible-centred. And this task is urgent! Only an adequate presentation of the message of the Scriptures can counteract this disturbing trend.

The Emerging Godless Generation in Africa

In Africa, it is presumed that age brings wisdom. Grey hair is regarded as evidence of wisdom gleaned from the experiences of life. That is why children are expected to follow the instructions of their parents. We find similar teaching about parents and their children in the Bible. For example, Proverbs 1:8 says, "Listen, my son, to your father's instruction and do not forsake your mother's teaching." Proverbs 3:1–2 says, "My son, do not forget my teaching, but keep my commands in your heart, for they will prolong your life many years and bring you prosperity."

However, not many children, even from religious homes, are enthusiastic about religion today. Not many of them bother to follow the footsteps of their godly parents. Some prefer to watch sports or play computer games rather than attend Sunday worship with their parents. Others pretend to be religious at home but act very differently when they are away from home, especially when they go to school as boarders. Sadly, children from Christian homes in Africa are more likely to come under the bad influence of their ungodly peers than the good influence of their parents. Some of these children have even joined occult groups and become a source of terror to their own parents.

At the seminary where I teach, there is a programme that trains youth workers. Recently, students in this programme were given a week to exhibit what they were learning in preparation for youth ministry. The theme of the week was "Do Something". In one session they discussed the factors responsible for youth waywardness. Several of them shared their personal testimonies. A recurring theme was that youth had experienced a lack of adequate attention from their parents – even from Christian parents. Sadly, this was even the case with those who were the children of pastors or priests.

This says a lot about parents. Some so-called Christian parents do not care about religion. Some of them do not even care about fellowship with other Christians. They prefer to stay home on Sundays and watch Christian television programmes on the Trinity or Daystar channels. Watching Christian television has become their version of having fellowship with God and with fellow believers. One wonders how exactly these parents are godly. Children from such homes are likely to learn these wrong attitudes to Christian fellowship from their parents.

We know that instructing children in the Scriptures lays a good foundation for their future lives. But modelling godly living for them and giving them enough attention are also very important. Christian parents will save their children from many dangers and themselves from many hurts if they do this. Therefore, biblical preaching in Africa should also concentrate on family issues. The message of the Bible is to be presented in a manner that is not only comprehensible but that can also be measured in order to assess growth. A conscious effort by Christian parents and the church working together at child training will save both the next generation of Christians and the quality of Christian spirituality in modern Africa.

What Is To Be done?

Ten years ago, I had an unforgettable experience when teaching a class in the seminary. As the class was ending, a female student protested, "Sir, I must talk to you." So I invited her to come to my office. When I asked what the matter was, she said she had been denied the opportunity to ask a question even when her hand was up. I apologized and explained that I had not seen her hand.

Just as this student thought it important to speak to the teacher about an issue that concerned her, so African Christians must also find it important to speak to their preachers about the need for Bible-centred preaching.

Serious preachers of the word of God must demonstrate their own commitment to biblical preaching. It should be the word of God, not the word of the preacher, that is heard in every sermon. And the God whose word is preached must be the God of the Bible, not the god of some other religion.

The antidote to the evils that are affecting our societies and our homes is the simple and clear preaching of the Bible with relevant application of its message to real life issues.

5

CHALLENGES TO BIBLICAL PREACHING IN AFRICA

Africa as a continent is facing many challenges including poverty, sickness and disease, ethnic and tribal conflicts, underdevelopment, poor education, poor public health services, and bad leadership. We are also seeing the rise of terrorist groups such as Al-Shabab and Boko Haram. These challenges are often obstacles to progress. What is true of Africa is also true of the church in Africa. It too has its share of challenges, and some of these challenges make it difficult for us to engage in evangelism and in biblical preaching.

Cultural Barriers to Communication

Patterns of communication vary from culture to culture. Even within one culture they may vary depending on whether you are talking to people who live in a city or in a rural area. If the way you present your message is unacceptable to your audience, they will not even hear the message, let alone consider accepting it. That is why all missionary training programmes include training on how to present the gospel in culturally appropriate ways that make it easier for people to accept.

We understand this in regard to missionaries coming into a foreign culture, but we sometimes forget that we too have cultural patterns of communication that can either obstruct or enhance the presentation of the Scriptures. For example, in Africa the old are highly respected and are thought to have more wisdom than the young. Thus the words of an elderly person are readily accepted and carry far more weight than those of a younger person. We learn this at an early age, when we are taught not to address our parents from a standing position, or to look them straight in the eyes, or to talk back to them when rebuked. Those are signs of disrespect. Depending on your culture, you may have been taught to crouch down, kneel, or squat when talking to your elders. You may even have been taught that it was disrespectful to ask your father something directly and told that you must ask your mother or an older sibling to approach your father on your behalf.

This cultural pattern of interaction can cause great problems for young preachers who are trying to present the gospel and to introduce biblical preaching in communities where it has not been known. It is very dangerous for young pastors to assume that because they are educated and bear the title of pastor, people will listen to what they have to say. Demanding that older people pay attention will only alienate them. One should never forget that age is respected in Africa.

So what can young preachers do when called to preach to older persons? How can they prevent their message from being rejected or not taken seriously because of their age? By remembering the cultural principles of respect you were taught as a child. A young preacher needs to speak humbly when presenting the Scriptures so that the message of God's word will be accepted.

Gender too can raise obstacles to biblical preaching. African culture does not grant women equal status with men. In some cultures, women squat with their head down when speaking to their husbands or to men. When a family problem needs to be resolved, a wife will often ask a relative to speak to her husband. These attitudes present a problem when a woman is the one presenting Scripture. Yet most men are willing to listen to a woman who is respectful and submissive, and who speaks kindly and gently. There is a female pastor and preacher in Abuja, Nigeria I respect and love to listen to preach. She demonstrates the attitude of respect and humility. A wise preacher will use this to her advantage when presenting the Scriptures, observing the community's norms of respect and communication while still proclaiming the truth.

Traditional customs must also be taken into consideration. If you go out to preach in a rural area, you need to remember that any activity that concerns a particular community must have the approval of community elders. Often a chief or village head is vested with the authority to make decisions on matters affecting the area, and must be approached indirectly, through lower traditional titleholders. Visitors to the village are expected to register their presence with the traditional head of the village to guarantee their security and obtain permission for any activities they plan to engage in. This means that a chief also controls the information that reaches the community, and can refuse permission to preach the Bible. Preachers who wish to have their message heard must show respect for constituted authorities and follow the approved cultural lines of communication if they are to negotiate successfully with traditional leaders.

Just as access to an African village is determined by its chief, so access to an African family is determined by the father, who is the head of the home and must be consulted before anything is done or any decision taken. In some homes, the father may not want to hear the message of the Bible, nor wish his family to receive it. This can be a great obstruction to presenting the message of the Scriptures within a family setting. However, even this obstacle can often be overcome by a child who shows obedience, respect and loyalty (Eph 6:1–3), and a wife who shows submission, respect and a gentle spirit (1 Pet 3:1–2; Eph 5:33). Persuasive negotiation can win the approval of a husband or father for the presentation of the Scriptures.

Lure of False Preachers

Many new churches are being started all over Africa, and many new "ministries" are emerging and attracting members from the mainline churches. These churches and ministries advertise their programmes on television, on the radio, on billboards and on signs along the roads. Some of them promise miracles and breakthroughs that will enable people to escape from sickness, poverty, witchcraft, untimely death, bad dreams and many other misfortunes.

Some of those who start these ministries are nothing but modernized witch doctors who have dressed themselves in the spiritual garment of Christianity but preach a religion of protection and prosperity rather than transformation. They distribute anointing oil, handkerchiefs, and other spiritual objects that are nothing but "Christianized" versions of traditional charms and amulets. They forget all about the Christian virtue of humility. Instead, they dress in expensive clothes and exert their authority as "children of the King". People are overawed by their vehicles, jewellery and clothing and believe what they say.

It is particularly easy for people to believe these false preachers because their practices are similar to those of authority figures in traditional African religions. But Christians who follow them are like the Jews who went looking for Jesus only because they wanted bread (John 6:25–27, 66–69). They are not looking for God and spiritual life but only for material blessings and physical protection.

We should not be surprised when we encounter such attitudes. The Apostle Paul predicted that people would abandon the truth and prefer falsehood (2 Tim 4:3–4). He would describe some of the preachers we see in Africa today as enemies of the cross because they distort the true gospel and see preaching as a way to wealth (2 Cor 2:17; Gal 1:6–7; Phil 1:15, 18).[1]

At times, even faithful preachers may be tempted by the material success of false preachers. We wonder whether we could enjoy the same luxuries if we just adjusted our message a bit. But biblical preachers must heed Paul's challenge to Timothy to "Preach the word; be prepared in season and out of season; correct, rebuke and encourage – with great patience and careful instruction" (2 Tim 4:2). Through God's strength, we should be willing to stand alone for the truth and preach the truth of the Bible even when no one wants to listen, and even when our church members decide to follow false preachers. Our attitude of humility and simplicity must stand in sharp contrast to the boasting of the false preachers.

Low Levels of Biblical Literacy

It has been said that the African version of Christianity is focused more on emotions than on careful thinking, implying that African Christians are not interested in critical reflection on what they hear. This observation

---

[1] For more on this, see Femi Adeleye, *Preachers of a Different Gospel* (Jos/Nairobi: Hippo, 2011).

is true of many today. They accept what they hear and do whatever a preacher tells them to do without first thinking it through and asking some basic questions.

One reason for this attitude is rooted in traditional African culture. Africans are not trained in the type of critical thinking that flourishes in the West. Instead, we are trained from childhood through proverbs and careful observation to learn to be wise in society. Moreover, many Africans grow up in communities where every member of the community is expected to be truthful and to uphold the value of honesty. Upright behaviour and attitudes are expected of all. People raised in such a context are not naturally suspicious of the words of others. They are accustomed to relying on others, particularly the elderly, for guidance when making decisions or resolving conflicts.

This traditional background influences the way people approach the matter of understanding the Scriptures. They do not bother to study the Scriptures for themselves. Instead they wait to be told what the Bible says by their pastor or priest. The more naïve among them will believe whatever they are told about the Bible since pastors or priests are expected to know the Bible and to speak the truth. Even among those Pentecostals who give time to studying the Scriptures and quote it in almost every conversation, some cannot say what the exact meaning of a passage is because they lack knowledge of some basic principles of interpretation. Sadly, this is true even of some pastors and preachers. Because they themselves lack biblical literacy, they are incapable of biblical preaching – and their failings when it comes to interpretation inevitably affect the quality of the Christian lives of those to whom they preach.

To produce a new generation of biblical preachers, we need to start by producing people who know their Bibles. Those of us who have been trained in theological schools should set about teaching those to whom we preach some simple principles of Bible interpretation. Those of us who have not had the privilege of theological education should take advantage of any seminars or courses like those offered by Langham Preaching that will give us ongoing training in biblical interpretation and preaching.[2] In fact, all of us, regardless of our level of education,

---

[2] For more on Langham Preaching, see http://langham.org/what-we-do/langham-preaching/

should welcome such courses to ensure that our knowledge remains fresh and our commitment steadfast. There is always more we can learn when it comes to understanding the Bible and knowing how to preach it.

When Christians are biblically literate, they are less likely to be misled by false teaching. They will learn not to accept everything that is said from the pulpit, but will be like the Christians in Berea, who tested what they heard by what is said in the Bible before they committed themselves to believing it (Acts 17:11). If African Christians did this, they would not be misled by false teachers. They would not heed those who interpret Christian giving as a commercial contract negotiated with God so that he can bless the giver. Instead, they will help to make sure that you as the preacher stay true to the teaching of the Bible.

Attack of the Enemy

The devil fights against what is good and godly. He began this with Adam and Eve in the Garden of Eden (Gen 3:1–7). Even when Jesus Christ came, the devil did all he could to stop him from going to the cross (Matt 2:1–10, 16–18; 4:1–11). He has always opposed God's plan for human salvation. Paul frequently mentions the attempts of the enemy of the cross to hamper his missionary work and the preaching of the gospel (Acts 13:6–12; 1 Tim 5:14–15; Phil 3:18–19).

One of the ways in which the devil works to achieve his goals is by discouraging biblical preaching and encouraging easy preaching for easy Christianity. He has been doing this sort of thing for a long time. In the days of the prophet Jeremiah the devil was encouraging false prophets to "dress the wound of my people as though it were not serious. 'Peace, peace,' they say, when there is no peace" (Jer 6:14; 8:11). Today, he is at work when pastors argue that because some church members no longer want to be confronted with the truth of the Bible, a preacher should give them what they want. "What they want" is not the liberating truth from Scripture but some tale that will make them laugh their sorrows away while their sin and spiritual blindness remain.

The enemy also loves to use vices such as bitterness, a desire for revenge, a lack of love, and a lack of forgiveness to cause cracks in the unity of the church. He takes steps to ensure that some pastors or priests do not see eye-to-eye with their colleagues. Still worse, he is diverting the attention of a growing number of them from the ministry into the struggle for material things. This shift has planted the spirit of competition among preachers. He has also encouraged dishonesty, laziness, falsehood, sexual immorality and the like among pastors and priests in Africa. Then he stirs in the poison of tribal loyalties, church politics, and the practice of having a godfather in the ministry to protect one's interest.

Responding to the Challenges

In this chapter we have looked at some of the huge challenges we face when we seek to practise biblical preaching in Africa. We have also considered some ways to handle these challenges. We are confident that they can all be overcome if we act wisely and stand on the truth of Scripture, as Jesus did.

Do you remember the incident described in John 6:22–69? It was the day after Jesus had fed thousands of people. Some of them tracked him down where he was preaching. They were very glad to find him, but were not interested in what he was saying; all they wanted was some more bread. But Jesus would not give them bread; instead he told them the hard truth, "Do not work for food that spoils, but for food that endures to eternal life". He wanted them to be looking for things that have eternal value. But they took offence at his teaching and left. Then Jesus asked his close disciples whether they too would leave him. Peter responded, "Lord, to whom shall we go? You have the words of eternal life. We have come to believe and to know that you are the Holy One of God."

The message Jesus preached was not the one people wanted to hear. But it was the one they needed to hear, for it came from God. In the same way, preachers in Africa must resist the temptation to tell people what they want to hear and must instead preach sermons that are rooted in the truths of the Bible.

As spiritual leaders, we need to return to the roots of our Christian heritage in Africa, remember the sacrifices made by those who handed down the faith to us, recall what God's judgement on unfaithful service will be like, and then pledge our loyalty to Jesus as Peter did. Thereafter, our first step must be to repent of our own sins and resolve to do what is right according to the Scriptures so that we can be examples to those around us. We cannot expect others to listen to biblical preaching if we do not ourselves submit to the authority of the Bible.

The only effective way to counter the attacks of the enemy on the church is to resolve to honour God and maintain our loyalty to him in thought, word, and deed.

6

PREPARING TO PREACH

If you were a farmer wanting to prepare a field for planting, the first thing you would have to do is take a good look at the field. You would have to assess what needs to be done before you could plant anything. Are there a lot of stones that must be cleared away? Are there trees that need to be cut down or preserved? Is the field overgrown with weeds? What type of crop would grow best in this field? You would also need to look inward and ask yourself, "Am I strong enough to do all the work that is needed to bring a crop in this field to harvest?"

The same type of preparation is needed if you are a preacher preparing to plant the seed of the word in your "field" or congregation. You cannot hope for a good harvest unless you have taken the trouble to think carefully about the field in which you are sowing the seed. You also need to think about how you will go about your work.

In this chapter, we will discuss some of the things you as a preacher need to be thinking about as you begin your sermon preparation. Or maybe, we should say that these are the things you should be conscious of as you prepare to start the work of sowing the word of God in the hearts and minds of your congregation.

Be Aware of What the Bible Is

Traditional African farmers use implements like ploughs, hoes, axes, machetes, sickles and axes. They know how and when to use each of these implements. They understand the importance of caring for their tools and knowing how to use them well. In a similar way, the Bible is the main tool or implement of the African preacher and so in order to be effective a preacher must understand it and know how to use it well.

So what is the Bible? It is the inspired word of God. It is inspired because those who wrote it, using human words so the Bible could be understood by people, were guided by God himself through his Holy Spirit. While he allowed them the freedom to choose what vocabulary to use and how to express themselves as they wrote, they were guided to write the exact message God wanted to communicate to his people.

But the Bible is not just one book. It is actually sixty-six books, joined together in one book. These sixty-six books are subdivided into the thirty-nine books that make up the Old Testament and the twenty-seven that make up the New Testament.

The thirty-nine books of the Old Testament are also subdivided into groups. The first five books (from Genesis to Deuteronomy) are known as the Pentateuch. They are followed by the Historical books (Joshua to Esther), the Wisdom books (Job to Song of Solomon) and the Prophetic books (Isaiah to Malachi). Similarly, the New Testament is divided into the four Gospels (Matthew to John), the Acts of the Apostles, and the Letters (Romans to Revelation). These groups of books have different styles and need to be interpreted differently. This is something you will need to study more if you want to be able to preach the Bible well. We do not have time to look at this in detail in this book, but at the end of the book you will find a list of some useful books that you can read to build up your knowledge of the Bible.

It is also important to remember that these sixty-six books were not all written at the same time, nor was each book written in just a few days, or even a few years. They were written by various authors at various times over a period of more than a thousand years. This means that the authors were not all writing in exactly the same historical period and the same circumstances. They each had to deal with the customs, culture, politics, economy, religion and social relationships existing in their time. When we recognize this, we realize why we need to learn more about the background information to each book. Knowing when each writer was writing, who he was writing to, and what circumstances they were in will help us explain the meaning of the Bible better and apply its message more appropriately to the issues of our own time.

You can now see why, if you want to be the best preacher you can possibly be, you need to apply yourself to learning more about the tool you use, the Bible.

Be Aware of the Need to Respect the Bible

The Bible must be respected by those who preach it. That is why a good preacher must cultivate an attitude of reverence for the Bible as the word of God. This respect is nothing like the so-called respect shown to the Bible by those who see it as a magic book that will protect them if they put it under their pillow. Those who do this are using the Bible, but they are not honouring it properly. They are thinking that it is a tool that they can use to manipulate God and force him to protect them. In other words, they are treating it as an idol. But God cannot be manipulated. The Bible is not a book to be worshipped, or a magic book or a charm; it is just a book.

But although the Bible is just a book, it is also far more than just a book. It is a religious book that contains the inspired word of God, the record of God's revelation of himself to human beings. The Bible helps us to know the mind and plans of God. God still speaks through it to us today. It is thus a book that should be treated with the respect and honour it deserves.

How do we show this respect? We do so in two ways. The first is the simplest. We show respect for the Bible by the way we handle our physical copies of the Bible. The way you hold your Bible will be interpreted by others as revealing your attitude to it. For example, some preachers fold one side of the Bible as they would an ordinary book when they are reading from it while preaching. Others use dusty and torn Bibles when preaching. If that is the only Bible you have, treat that torn Bible with dignity. But if you have other Bibles, bring your best Bible into the pulpit with you. Let the congregation see that you honour God's word. Then they too will respect it as the word of God and be ready to listen to preaching from it with an attitude of reverence.

But it is not enough just to put on an outward show of our reverence for the Bible. Any actor can do the same. You need to show your respect for the Bible in the way you study it, the way you preach from it, and the way you talk about it to your congregation. You should approach your study of the Bible and your preaching with fear and reverence. All true and serious preachers, even those who have had almost no training in theology, know that the Bible as the word of God functions as the final authority in matters of faith and as a guidebook for life. In it God speaks to people about himself and themselves. Every opinion or argument is subject to the Bible as the final authority and judge.

As Africans, we know how to show respect for traditional rulers in the way we talk about them, the way we greet them, and the way we behave when in their presence. Why would we show less respect for God's word? If we do, the message others will get from us is that the Bible is not worth listening to. In that case, they will also see no point in listening to a sermon based on the Bible. Your people will start to assume that if the word of God in the Bible can be disrespected, there is no need to respect and obey the God of the Bible.

As a preacher, you must always remember that people watch you and follow your example. Some of them even act out what they see and hear from you. Do not be a bad example to them. Respect the Bible, treat it with dignity, and preach it well with conviction, passion, sincerity and devotion.

Be Aware of Your Spiritual Responsibilities

When I was a young boy growing up in a village, it was my responsibility to cut grass every day to feed our animals. When I became a pastor, I became responsible for feeding people spiritually through my preaching. That spiritual responsibility is a far heavier burden than any physical responsibilities I have ever had! And just as I needed to be physically healthy to carry out my physical responsibilities, so I need to be spiritually healthy to be able to carry out my spiritual responsibilities.

How does one become spiritually healthy? One of the first steps is to avoid spiritual "germs" and "wounds". As we saw in chapter five, the devil will always attack anything that is godly and any activity that is done to honour God. The only way we can avoid spiritual injury is by using the spiritual protection that God provides. Remember Paul's advice to the Christians in Ephesus:

Put on the full armour of God, so that you can take your stand
against the devil's schemes. For our struggle is not against flesh
and blood, but against the rulers, against the authorities, against
the powers of this dark world and against the spiritual forces of
evil in the heavenly realms. Therefore put on the full armour
of God, so that when the day of evil comes, you may be able
to stand your ground, and after you have done everything, to
stand. Stand firm then, with the belt of truth buckled around
your waist, with the breastplate of righteousness in place, and
with your feet fitted with the readiness that comes from the
gospel of peace. In addition to all this, take up the shield of
faith, with which you can extinguish all the flaming arrows of
the evil one. Take the helmet of salvation and the sword of the
Spirit, which is the word of God.

And pray in the Spirit on all occasions with all kinds of
prayers and requests. With this in mind, be alert and always
keep on praying for all the Lord's people. (Eph 6:11–18; see
also Rom 13:11–14)

We need the whole armour of God if we are to survive spiritual battles,
and we need to fight those battles with the spiritual strength that only
the Holy Spirit gives. While this is true for all Christians, it is especially
important for pastors, who are on the frontline of the battle. Despite
the constant demands made on us as pastors, we need to make sure
that we remain spiritually fit and ready for battle by making time for
serious personal Bible study, prayer and fasting. We should never be
casual about our own devotional life.

Be Aware of the Spiritual Condition of Your Audience

Each time we preach, we must be aware that not everyone listening
to us is a Christian. Some in the congregation may not yet have been
converted, and others may even have been sent by the devil to disrupt
the service and distract the people from what you are saying so that they
do not hear God's word to them. This truth was confirmed to me by

someone I know well who was once deeply involved in occult practices. He testified that agents from the occult world are sent to many places, including churches, to sow havoc, confusion and pain.

A preacher who is truly convinced about the power of the Bible will not take the spiritual condition of the audience lightly. For this reason, preachers must spend much time in prayer, knowing that our enemy the devil will seek to disrupt our preparation, our preaching of God's word, and the response of the listeners.

But we do not preach only to non-believers. We also preach to believing members of the congregation. Some of them are going through difficult times because of their personal, family or work circumstances, or because of something that is going on in the community or the nation. In Nigeria, for example, there have been many attacks by the terrorist group known as Boko Haram and there is an economic recession. Such things affect the congregation, and we need to be aware of them if we want what we say to be relevant to our hearers' lives.

Speaking of this aspect of preparing to preach, John Stott used to say that a biblical preacher should engage in "double listening". We should listen to what people are saying, both in the words they say and the way they live, and listen to what God is saying in his word. Then we can build a bridge that brings these two things together.[1]

Let me give you an example of what I mean. Suppose you live in an area where many of the people are thieves in one way or another. You probably want to preach a sermon rebuking them and condemning stealing. But before doing that, you need to listen to the people and find out why they are stealing. Is it because they are greedy or covetous, or is it because they are starving, or is it because things were stolen from them? Once you know the answer to that question, you will have a much better idea of how to present what the Bible says and to address what is wrong.

To give another example, if you discover that many people in your area are engaged in sexual immorality, first find out why they are doing this before presenting what the Bible says about it. Are women being

---

[1] For more on this, see John Stott and Greg Scharf, *I Believe in Preaching* (Carlisle: Langham Preaching Resources, 2013 / Grand Rapids: Eerdmans, 2015). See also John Stott, *The Contemporary Christian* (Leicester: IVP, 1995).

forced into prostitution because they have been widowed or abandoned by their husbands? Is this the only way they can get money to feed their children? If so, your preaching must deal not only with sexual morality but also with the responsibilities of husbands to their wives, and with the need for the congregation to find practical ways to help those in deep poverty.

Be Aware of the Reward for Faithful Stewardship

Pastors who are faithful in preaching will benefit from both present and future rewards. Our earthly rewards include people appreciating our preaching and the way we carry out our other pastoral duties and praying for us (2 Cor 9:12–14). We need such prayers just as much as the Apostle Paul did when he asked Christians to pray for him (Eph 6:18–20; Phil 1:19–20). People will sometimes encourage us with kind words and with gifts of money, clothing, food, and so on that help to meet our material needs. We will also enjoy respect if our ministry is characterized by faithfulness and integrity. In some congregations, the pastor is honoured by being referred to as a father while his wife is seen as the mother of the congregation.

But even more important than the rewards of respect and support is the reward of seeing the effects of your preaching in the lives of people. Paul knew this joy well. He had spent some time pastoring the church in Ephesus, and when he later wrote to them he said, "Ever since I heard about your faith in the Lord Jesus and your love for all God's people, I have not stopped giving thanks for you, remembering you in my prayers" (Eph 1:15–16). Writing to the Christians in Philippi, Paul called them "my joy and my crown" (Phil 4:1). It is indeed rewarding to see people you have mentored directly and indirectly through your pastoral and preaching ministry doing well in the faith.

I know this personally, for some of the many students I have taught are doing very well in ministry. This is my joy, satisfaction and reward as a teacher. While they see me as their mentor, I see them as the reward of my teaching ministry.

There are also eternal rewards for pastors and all others who have been faithful in doing what God has required of them. They will enjoy eternal crowns and a place in heaven (John 14:1–3) on the day when Jesus will say, "Well done, good and faithful servant! . . . Come, you who are blessed by my Father; take your inheritance, the kingdom prepared for you" (Matt 25:23, 34; Rev 22:12–14).

Our awareness of the reward for faithful pastoral ministry, and especially for faithful preaching of the word of God, should encourage us in the work of ministry.

When we do our work well, we are blessed. But the opposite is also true as the following story illustrates: There was once a stingy king who gave a blind beggar a snake instead of alms. The king's son, who was envious and equally stingy, saw his father putting something large in the beggar's pocket and assumed it was a large sum of money. He wanted to get that money back. So he quickly put his own hand inside the beggar's pocket – and was promptly bitten by the poisonous snake. He died in agony. When the beggar realized what had happened, he told the king: "Oh king, if you do what is good, you will find blessing; if you do what is evil, you will find destruction." This same truth applies to us as preachers. If we are unfaithful to our calling to proclaim his word, we will face the judgement of God.

Sometimes we are tempted to become careless and allow our devotion, dedication and commitment to pastoral ministry and the work of preaching to slide. At such times, we should remind ourselves that in the Old Testament, we are told, "Whatever your hand finds to do, do it with all your might" (Eccl 9:10). In the New Testament we are told "whatever you do, do it all for the glory of God" (1 Cor 10:31). Jesus told a parable about someone who failed to do this – the parable of the Talents (Matt 25:14–30). In that parable, a faithful servant who was given five talents gained five more through trading. Another faithful servant also doubled the talents he was given. Not so the third servant. He did nothing with the gift he had been given, wasting his opportunity for service, and was severely reprimanded for being wicked and lazy.

Like the servants in the parable, we pastors will one day have to give a report on our service. On that day, all preachers – the faithful and unfaithful, the zealous and committed, the lazy, the serious, the passionate and the humorous – will be judged and rewarded according to how they treated the word of God, how they preached the Bible, and whether or not they were faithful in interpreting and teaching it.

So we should heed Paul's instruction to the young pastor Timothy, which I will repeat because it is so important: "Preach the word; be prepared in season and out of season; correct, rebuke and encourage – with great patience and careful instruction" (2 Tim 4:2). We will have no excuse when we stand before God. We will not be able to tell him that it was "inconvenient" to spend time in prayer and preparation before we preached.

7

DECIDING WHAT TO PREACH

In the last chapter, we looked at things you need to be aware of in regard to your role as a preacher. But that chapter did not give any practical advice on how to go about preparing or preaching a sermon. That is what we will be looking at in more detail in the next few chapters.

You may find it helpful to think about this process in terms of the way we build a house. First, we decide on the location, then we lay a foundation, then we put up walls, then we install the rafters, and finally we attach the roof. These are the basic steps and they apply to whatever type of house we are building – whether a traditional mud-walled dwelling with a grass roof, a house made with cement blocks and a corrugated iron roof, or a mansion. In the same way, these steps should be part of the process of preparing every sermon you preach. The sermons you build may be as different from one another as the different types of houses are, but they all need foundations, walls and a roof!

Just as building a house takes planning and work, so does crafting a sermon. Sermons don't just happen. They don't come to us by magic, and we cannot simply rely on last-minute inspiration as we walk to church or step into the pulpit. (Jesus' words in Luke 21:12–15 about not worrying beforehand about what to say relate to what to say when we are being attacked by others, not to what to say when we preach and teach.) No, building a sermon involves work, and there are certain steps to be followed if we want to be workers who produce a sermon we will not be ashamed of when we think back on it. We need to work at correctly handling the word of truth (see 2 Tim 2:15).

The Idea for a Sermon

We have already said that a sermon must be based on the Bible – but on what part of the Bible? The Bible is a huge book. How do we decide which passage to preach from on any particular Sunday? Do we just open the Bible at random and choose the first verse we see as the topic for our sermon? Well, would you choose the location for a house that way? No. We spend time considering where we should build our house, and the same is true when we are considering where to build our sermon.

Or do you just try and find a verse that speaks to you in your own devotions that week and then preach on that? There is nothing wrong with this, but it may be a little like building a house in a place where you like the view, without considering important details like how you will get a road to the door and provide water to this hilltop site (or whether a site in a beautiful valley is prone to flooding when the rains come).

Just as you have to investigate the location and draw up a plan before starting to build your house, so you have to prayerfully consider where to locate your sermon. What is it that the congregation needs to know? That is what you should be preaching about.

This is where "double listening" is important. By listening to your congregation, you will have developed some understanding of their needs. You will know whether this is a time when they need to be comforted, or encouraged, or challenged. You will know about problems within the congregation, or in the economy or in politics, or challenging family issues such as the relationship between a husband and wife, parenting, or the interference of extended family members. Or you may be seeing the negative influence of the media, pornography, and the wrong use of social media. Or you may just be seeing people treating each other badly. All of these suggest possibilities for sermons.

But you do not only listen to your congregation. You also need to listen to God's word. Your goal as a pastor is to help the congregation know what God has said in his word, and in all of his word, both in the Old and New Testaments. So sometimes you may need to preach on passages that teach important truths that your congregation needs to know, regardless of whether there is a pressing need to preach on them at that time. It helps if people know a truth before a crisis strikes rather than struggling to understand it as the floods of trouble roar around them.

Sometimes, it is relatively easy to know the general topic we should be preaching on. Christmas, Easter, Palm Sunday, and so on are very important times in the church, and we should probably use them to preach on passages that relate to these events in the life of Christ. Our goal should be to help the congregation understand more deeply what these events mean for us and for the world.

There may also be other important annual events in your congregation such as First Fruits Sundays, Harvest Thanksgiving, Revival Service(s), Fathers' Day and Mothers' Day, Couples' Week, and so on. For those Sundays, you choose Bible passages that are relevant to these occasions and help your congregation to learn what God says about these aspects of life.

But such events cover maybe ten Sundays a year. What are you going to preach about on the other forty-two Sundays? How are you going to give your congregation a balanced biblical diet over those weeks? Will you have to spend the first half of each week worrying about what to preach on the following Sunday? Is that an effective use of your preparation time? Surely not, because it means you will spend more time worrying about what to preach than actually studying the passage you plan to preach on. Some better plan is needed.

Some denominations help pastors answer the question about what to preach by following a yearly plan, so that preachers know which texts are to be preached on every Sunday of the year. Other denominations may choose one theme for a whole year, and suggest books and passages that you can preach on to develop that theme. Both these approaches can be helpful. But what do you do if you are not in one of those denominations?

One option is to make a list of all the Sundays in the coming year, or in the coming quarter if a year seems too long a span of time to consider. Mark off the dates when your topic is set by some event in the church year, and then prayerfully consider what you should be preaching on the remaining Sundays. Remember that you want to provide a balance of teaching from both the Old and New Testaments, from familiar texts as well as unfamiliar ones, and that you need to address both popular and unpopular themes (it is unwise only to preach on the subjects you love!). Your aim is that over the months (and years) in which you preach, your hearers will gradually come to an understanding of the whole of God's word.

By the time you have finished, you should have a set of ideas for sermons for the entire quarter (or even year). These are equivalent to the plans for your house. You now have plenty of time to start thinking and praying about these plans before they become a reality. Your sermon preparation is starting weeks before you have to preach the sermon!

Note that having a preaching schedule like this does not mean that you cannot change your plans in light of events in your community. Disasters and scandals and current events do sometimes need to be addressed in our sermons. But even when preaching on such topics, the Bible must be your main source and guide. Prayerfully seek God's guidance about which Bible passage you should use and how to apply it to the current situation. Your sermon should be based on the Bible, not the newspapers.

One final warning: remember that not everything that seems like a good idea for a sermon comes from God. There was a preacher in Nigeria about twenty-five years ago who had what he thought was a brilliant idea for a sermon: He would preach that God had told him to ask the congregation to enter into a special covenant or pact with him. Each member was to pay a specific amount of money every month as his or her covenant with God. This was in addition to their monthly tithes and Sunday offerings. By entering into this covenant, the people would attract God's blessings. But this idea for a sermon does not come from God because there is no way to justify it from the Bible.

The Kind of Sermon

When we lay out the floor plan of a modern house, we don't want every room to be exactly the same size. Some need to be larger, and others smaller. A bathroom does not have to be the same size as a living room or a kitchen. Even in the villages, the storehouses and the rooms for children and for adults do not have the same size and shape. Variety is needed if a house is to function well.

It has even been said that "variety is the spice of life", meaning that something new has a way of adding freshness to life. A new dance step, for example, spices up the excitement of the dancers. It feels good to wear a new article of clothing in a new style. The same is true when it comes to preaching. It is good to preach a variety of kinds of sermons.

When there is variety it adds to the interest of the listener in the word of God and in discussion about what God says in the Bible. The only thing that cannot vary in our sermons is that they must all be rooted in the Bible and must ultimately point to the God of the Bible.

Yet even that requirement allows for a great deal of variety because the Bible itself is full of variety. It includes history, poetry, biographies and stories, proverbs, prophecies and letters. These different formats lend themselves to different kinds of sermons.

Another source of variety in our preaching comes when we decide that some of our sermons will be single sermons while others will be part of a series. If they are part of a series, you can vary how long the series lasts. Sometimes a series may last for only two weeks (for example, a series on marriage in which you address husbands in one sermon and wives in the next). Sometimes it may last for a month (for example, a series on the book of Ruth, in which you preach on one chapter at a time). And sometimes a sermon series may last seven weeks (for example, if you are preaching on the letters to the seven churches at the start of Revelation). A series may last even longer than that if you and your congregation are going to be studying a whole book like the Gospel of Mark, but in that case you may want to break up the long series with a few stand-alone sermons on a particular topic or by spending a week or two on some different short series from a different part of Scripture.

Sermons can also vary by being either expository or topical. The first example that I gave above is an example of a topical sermon series. The preacher was addressing the topic of marriage. In topical preaching, the sermon focuses on a particular issue (like marriage, or corruption, or wealth, or holiness) and explores what the Bible has to say about it. This is a very popular kind of sermon or sermon series and it can be very effective.

With topical sermons, however, we have to be very careful to ensure that the focus remains on what the Bible says and not on our ideas about the topic. We must avoid the temptation to take verses out of context and use them to support our opinion. That is called proof-texting. When we do that, we are reading our own meaning into the text rather than listening to what the text itself says. The congregation should hear what God says from the Bible as you develop the sermon.

A topical sermon that is based on a right understanding of the Scriptures is a good and helpful form of preaching. You can see an example of such a sermon in Appendix 2, in the sermon where I address the topic of caring for pastors so that they and their families do not fall into poverty. When you read that sermon, you will see that my presentation of the topic is rooted in a particular passage from the Bible.

Biographical sermons are a special category of topical sermons (or sermon series). In a biographical sermon, the preacher speaks about the life or experiences of a Bible character (like David, or Ruth, or Paul) and then draws lessons from that person's life and applies them to the listener. Appendix 2 to this book includes two examples of biographical sermons, one dealing with King Jehoshaphat in the Old Testament and the other with the Apostle Paul in the New Testament.

In preparing a topical sermon we begin with a topic or a character, and set out to preach on that. But when it comes to an expository sermon (or sermon series) we don't first choose a subject and then look for it in the Bible. Instead, the subject of our sermon emerges as we study the Bible. You could say that an expository sermon is one that 'exposes' the Scriptures. We are not looking for what we can say about some topic, but for what the Bible itself has to say about the topics God thinks are important. So when we preach an expository sermon, we start with a Scripture. For example, we may study our Lord's teaching in the Sermon on the Mount, or his parables, or the story of the Exodus, or a group of psalms. We will examine this passage of Scripture very carefully, and help our hearers understand what these words meant to the people who first heard them and what they mean to us today. In such a sermon, the topic and the outline of the sermon are not decided in advance but emerge from the Bible passage being studied. As you read on, you will learn more about how to prepare an expository sermon, and you will see several examples of expository sermons.

Preaching different types of sermons will help people to see the different ways God has related to people in history and will help them to experience the different ways they can encounter God in his word. But you should always remember that while it is the Bible that determines what we preach, the different experiences and conditions of people in the congregation determine what and how we apply the message of the Bible to them.

Pray

Given all the possible ideas you could preach on, and all the options in regard to sermon style, you may be feeling overwhelmed about how to decide what to preach on. That is why you need to pray before you prepare, while you prepare, after you prepare and before you preach.

Earlier, I compared preparing to preach to getting ready to go out to the farm to till the land and to building a house. But in reality preaching is very different from weeding out grasses or preparing a building site. It is not a physical activity but a spiritual activity. That is why we need spiritual preparation before we can preach. That is why prayer is the first step, and an ongoing necessity, in sermon preparation.

Praying about sermon preparation is not casual prayer but specific and intensive prayer that should involve some time for fasting as well. We should ask God for wisdom, knowledge, and understanding and for the guidance of his Holy Spirit as we choose a passage, as we study it, and for every step in the preparation and preaching of the sermon.

For example, you may have an idea that you want to preach about. Yet, it is possible that your sermon idea may not be what God wants a particular audience to hear at that particular time. That is why we need to pray for God's direction to help us identify what our people's needs are, what specific sermon idea we should nurture and how we should present it.

As the sermon preparation progresses, we need to also be praying for the audience. Those who listen to sermons come from different cultural backgrounds and have different needs and issues confronting them in life. These people come to church expecting that the day's sermon will help address those needs. We should be praying that God in his sovereign power will use the same sermon to address these various needs. For example, we should be praying that the hurting members of the congregation will find healing, the troubled and wounded ones will find his peace and comfort, those who are discouraged will find confidence, and the insecure will find assurance through the sermon.

We should also be praying for God to open our own eyes to see good sermon illustrations that will be relevant and appropriate to our audience. When we find such illustrations in the events around us, they can serve as bridges connecting the ancient text to the modern context and preparing the way for the application of the message in the sermon.

8

STUDYING THE SCRIPTURE

God has not called you to be a preacher so that you can tell the congregation what you think; he wants you to teach them about what he thinks. He has revealed his thinking to us in his word, the Bible, and so Christian preaching must be rooted in the Bible. It is our source, foundation, tool and authority. That is why you must pray not only about what topic you should preach on but what passage from the Bible you should base your sermon on.

Once you are sure what passage of Scripture you are going to be preaching on, you need to study that passage prayerfully and carefully to make sure that you understand what it says. We must not be like the man who preached on the story of Abraham's hospitality which includes the words, "Sarah laughed". The preacher read those words and assured the congregation, "Someone will laugh today!" Since people like to be happy, his audience chorused, "Amen", and began jumping and dancing.

That preacher's application shows that he had not taken the trouble to read the passage carefully. He missed the point that Sarah's laughter was not sparked by joy, hope or celebration. Rather, it was cynical, mocking laughter because she did not believe what the angel was saying. If you doubt this, read the passage:

> Abraham and Sarah were already very old, and Sarah was past the age of childbearing. So Sarah laughed to herself as she thought, "After I am worn out and my Lord is old, will I now have this pleasure?"

> Then the LORD said to Abraham, "Why did Sarah laugh and say, 'Will I really have a child, now that I am old?' Is anything too hard for the LORD? I will return to you at the appointed time next year, and Sarah will have a son."
>
> Sarah was afraid, so she lied and said, "I did not laugh."
>
> But he said, "Yes, you did laugh." (Gen 18:11–15)

When we misinterpret Scripture, we deceive and mislead the people who are listening to us. Some may stray into heresy. None of us wants to be the path by which errors enter the church. That is why we need to be very careful when interpreting Scripture. We must do our best to understand every aspect of the passage we are preaching on. Only then can we interpret it correctly.

The following questions are the ones we need to be able to answer if we are to be able to interpret a passage correctly:

- What did this passage mean to the people who first heard those words thousands of years ago?
- What does this passage mean in the context of the whole Bible?
- How does the message in this passage apply to life today?

While those questions seem simple, it takes a lot of work to find the answers to them. You will have to be a bit like a farmer who digs up a field in order to harvest yams, cassava, potatoes, or cocoyam to feed his family. Similarly, you will have to dig deep into the Bible text so that you understand exactly what it means. You can then use this knowledge to provide healthy spiritual food for those you preach to.

Read and Reread the Passage

After praying for the help of God's Spirit, you should sit down and start to really get to know the passage that you are going to be preaching on. Read it carefully, and read the chapters on either side of it too, so that you know the context in which this passage occurs. Write down anything that strikes you as you read.

Then read the passage again and again. Read it in as many different translations as you can find.[1] Read it in a number of different English translations, such as the English Standard Version (ESV), the New English Translation (NET), the New International Version (NIV), the New King James Version (NKJV), and the New Revised Standard Version (NRSV). If you are more comfortable reading in French or Portuguese, read more than one French or Portuguese translation. And of course you should also read it in your mother tongue, and in any other languages you know.

Why do I recommend reading so many different translations? The reason is that the Bible was not written in any one of the languages I have mentioned. The Old Testament was written mainly in Hebrew, and the New Testament mainly in Greek. So all the versions of the Bible that we have access to are translations from those languages into the languages we speak. As you can see when you look at the number of English language translations, these translations have been published to meet the needs of different groups of readers, even if they all speak the same language.

In Africa, most of us speak several languages, and so we have no difficulty with the idea of translation. We understand that different languages say things in different ways. Sometimes, we find it easier to say something in one language rather than another, because there is no word in the other language that captures our exact meaning. The translators of the Bible face exactly the same problem. They too do not always find it easy to translate a Hebrew or Greek word into another language. Sometimes they also had to translate words that can have more than one meaning. Different translators may have decided to translate that word in different ways.

When you read a number of translations, you will see how different translators have understood the passage and tried to convey its meaning. This will deepen your own understanding of the passage. You will be able to tell which ideas are central to the passage, because all the translators agree on them. You may also find that one translation of the passage

---

[1] If you have access to the Internet, you will see that Web sites like Biblegateway.com offer free access to many different translations of the Bible. If you do not have access to the Internet, you can consult a parallel Bible, that is, a Bible that has up to four different translations, printed in parallel on the page.

puts things in a way that your congregation will really understand, and decide to use that wording in your sermon. So keep notes as you read, jotting down points that strike you, and asking questions about things that puzzle you.

The number of times the passage should be read will vary from person to person. People differ in the speed of their reading and their ability to grasp the meaning of what they read, and some passages are more difficult to understand than others. The point is that this process should not be hurried. Take the time you need to grasp the meaning of the passage as this is the foundation on which the entire sermon will be built.

Ask Questions

As you read and reread a Bible passage in the same version or in different versions, you will find yourself starting to ask questions about specific parts of what you are reading. For instance, you may notice that some words are only used once while others are used repeatedly. You may be struck by certain phrases or expressions in the passage and wonder why they are used. You may wonder why the people in the passage are behaving in the way they do. What happened earlier that prompted their reactions? What were the consequences of their reactions?

These questions are important in helping you interpret the passage which, as we said earlier, means finding out what the passage meant to those who first heard it, what it means in the context of the whole Bible, and how it applies to our lives today.

You will, of course, come up with your own questions about the particular passage you are reading. But there are also some standard questions that you should ask about every passage you plan to teach on:

What type of writing is this passage?
We all know the difference between a song that celebrates victory in war or praises a hero, a song of lament by a childless woman, and a song that mourns the death of a loved one. These are all different genres of songs.

Similarly, there are different genres of writing. When we read our daily newspapers, we recognize the difference between the advertisements and the news reports. We know that a poetic account of a battle will not be the same as a historical account of what happened. We know that a leader will be described differently by a praise singer from the way he is described by a journalist or a historian. We understand that the poetic elements in the praise song are not to be taken literally but are imaginative ways to help us understand the ruler's greatness.

So when we start to study a passage of Scripture we need to ask ourselves, "What type of writing is this?" Or in other words, "what genre of writing am I reading?" It is not enough just to say that this type of writing is "the Bible", because the various writers who wrote the books of the Bible wrote in different genres. Sometimes they wrote poems and songs, sometimes they told stories about people or wrote histories, and sometimes they recorded proverbs or sayings that encapsulate some general truth. This is true not only of whole books (e.g. Leviticus is a book of laws, while Psalms is a poetry book) but also within books. A book that is written mainly in one genre may include passages that are written in a different genre (e.g. the book of 2 Samuel is a history of David's reign, but it also includes a song in the first chapter and a parable in chapter 12).

It is very important for us to understand this as preachers, because the genre of the passage we are reading affects the way we read it, the way we interpret it and the way we preach it. Let me give you some examples of what I mean.

- When we preach on Paul's letters to the Ephesians, we can tell husbands to love their wives, because that is clearly an instruction that the apostle is issuing to all Christians.

- When we are preaching about Elijah, we need to recognize that this is a story about how God worked with one person, at one particular time in history. We should not tell our hearers to act in exactly the same way as Elijah did. We should not exhort them to call down fire from heaven or to slaughter false priests, as Elijah did at Mount Carmel. Instead, we must look for the general principles that lie behind the story rather than focusing on the surface details.

- When we preach on Revelation, we must recognize that it is not written as a history book to be interpreted literally but is an example of an unusual type of writing called "apocalyptic writing", which uses symbols and numbers to explain truths.

- When we preach on a book like Proverbs, we must recognize that the writer is expressing general truths, but that these do not apply in every single case. For example, it is generally true that a son should listen to his father, as Proverbs exhorts, but what if the father is exhorting the son to return to the ways of African Traditional Religion? Similarly, Psalm 1 presents the general truth that those who are godly will be blessed, but it should not be read as implying that someone who is poor and suffering is ungodly. A quick look at some of the other psalms in which the godly psalmist speaks of his own suffering will soon dispel that idea.

You may find it helpful to think of the idea of genre in terms of music. We love African music, and we know that different types of songs have different drumbeats and require different dance styles. The same is true of the Bible. Different parts of it have a different drumbeat and our "dance" or sermon must reflect that.

Who wrote this passage?

We do not always know who wrote each book in the Bible, for the human authors did not always sign their work. But if we can identify the author of a book, it may help us understand the meaning better. For example, when we read "I urge you to imitate me" (1 Cor 4:16), it helps to know that the "me" is the Apostle Paul. Our knowledge of Paul's life and of the relationship between him and the Christians in Corinth gives us insight into why he can say something like this and what action he wanted the Corinthians to take.

Who was the author writing to and why was he writing to them?

The different books of the Bible were written in very different periods. So some parts (particularly the first five books of the Bible) were addressed to people who were migrants, wandering around looking for a place to settle. Others were addressed to free people living in cities like Jerusalem and Rome, while others were written to people who have been carried off into captivity.

So it can be very helpful to try to learn something about the background to the book and the lifestyle of the people at the time the book was written. What type of food did they eat? What type of community did they live in? How did they farm, fight, marry, raise children, and so on? The more real these people are to you, the more you will be able to see the similarities and differences between them and the people to whom you are preaching. Recognizing these similarities and differences will, in turn, help you to come up with much better applications of the passage.

Where can you find this information? Some of it can be found as you read the Bible itself, but you can also find out more by looking up "life in Bible times" on the Internet or in books.

What is the context of this passage?

In traditional Africa, people lived close to members of their extended family, and were part of a larger community or clan. These communities were the context in which the people lived. When you met someone you did not know, you inquired about their family, clan and village, and that told you something about them. In the same way, every passage of Scripture has a context. Its "extended family" are the surrounding verses and chapters, and its "clan" is the entire book. Knowing something about the family and the neighbours will help to shed light on the meaning of the chosen passage, paragraph, verse, or even part of a verse. Their closeness makes them share certain things in common. That is why many writers on the subject of Bible interpretation tell us that context helps us to determine the meaning of a passage. It also helps us to preach the Bible correctly and apply it appropriately. We saw an example of the failure to look at context in the story about Sarah that opened this chapter.

How does this passage fit in to the theology of the whole Bible?

Do not be scared by the word "theology". Here I am using it simply to refer to what the Bible teaches about God, Jesus Christ, human beings, how to live the Christian life, death and the life after death, and other such topics. Biblical theology attempts to understand the teachings of the various books of the Old Testament and those of the New Testament and see how they are related. For example, how do Old Testament stories that involve polygamy and divorce relate to the New Testament understanding of marriage? And how does what the New Testament says about sin and punishment relate to the Old Testament laws?

Example of asking questions

I have just discussed some general questions that apply to every passage, but there are also specific questions that will arise in your own mind as you read and reread the passage you are going to preach on. Let me demonstrate what I mean by sharing the questions and answers that came to my mind as I read and reread the following passage in preparation for preaching on it.

> From this time many of his disciples turned back and no longer followed him.
>
> "You do not want to leave too, do you?" Jesus asked the Twelve.
>
> Simon Peter answered him, "Lord, to whom shall we go? You have the words of eternal life. We have come to believe and to know that you are the Holy One of God."(John 6:66–69)

I begin with the questions I know the answer to: Who wrote this book and why? We know that it was written by the Apostle John, and he tells us why he wrote it:

> Jesus performed many other signs in the presence of his disciples, which are not recorded in this book. But these are written that you may believe that Jesus is the Messiah, the Son of God, and that by believing you may have life in his name. (John 20:30–31)

That answer may influence how I interpret and preach on this passage because I see that there are two important links between these two passages. Both talk about "life", and both mention titles when they speak of Jesus. It is possible that the title Peter uses, "the Holy One of God" (6:69) may mean the same as "the Messiah, the Son of God" (20:31)? I will need to investigate this. The focus on "life" also means that this is an important theme in the book, and throws light on why it is important that people don't stop following Jesus.

Then I ask, what type of writing is this? The answer is that the verses I am looking at are clearly part of a narrative (story). So as I read them, I need to ask the questions that I would ask of any story: What is going on here? What happened before this, and what happened next? So I will have to read the whole of John 6 before I can preach on the closing verses.

But before I do that, I come up with some more detailed questions about the three verses I am looking at. Then I will know what background or context of the story I am looking for. For example, What does "this time" refer to? What had happened just before Jesus spoke these words? And before that? Why were all these people with Jesus? What had he been saying or doing? And what happened next?

I also need to ask questions about the identity of the participants: Who are the people involved in the story? Who were the many disciples who left Jesus? Why did others stay with him? What was the difference between the two groups that made them react so differently? Why was Peter the only one who answered Jesus' question? What happened to the other disciples who went away from Jesus?

I also need to ask questions about what was happening and why. What prompted those disciples to leave Jesus? Why did Jesus ask the Twelve, "You do not want to leave too, do you?" Why did Peter give the answer he did?

Finally, I need to ask questions about the concepts in this passage. Why are the people who left Jesus still referred to as "disciples" if they stopped following him? What does it mean to be a disciple? What did Peter mean when he said "You have the words of eternal life"? What is "eternal life"?

You will see that I have not yet worked out the answers to those questions. Nor do I yet know how those answers will fit together in a sermon. All that I am trying to do at this stage is make sure that I really understand the passage I am going to preach on.

Some of these questions may be fairly easy for you to answer, others may be difficult to answer on your own. In that case, you may find it helpful to consult a Study Bible that includes notes or to read what a Bible commentary has to say about the passage you are going to preach on. You may not be able to afford a whole set of commentaries, but even a one-volume commentary on the whole Bible like the *Africa Bible*

Commentary, will be an invaluable help in your preparation. It is worth saving up to buy one.[2]

Take Notes As You Read

Note-taking is a very important exercise when preparing every sermon. It helps you to keep track of ideas and thoughts that come to mind, and some of your notes will be very helpful when it comes to constructing your sermon.

What sort of things should you note? A good starting point would be to jot down the standard questions mentioned above, and any other questions that come into your mind as you read. Then write down the answers that you find to those questions. Also, note any thoughts, applications or images that come into your mind as you reflect on what you have been reading.

Let me give you an example of some of the notes I might have jotted down as I was studying John 6:66–69:

Background questions: The immediate "neighbourhood" of John 6:66–69 is the whole chapter. When I read John 6, I found that a great crowd of people had followed Jesus because of his healing miracles. Then he had performed yet another miracle when he fed about five thousand of them from only five loaves of bread and two fish. It seems possible that many of the people were following him around because they wanted another free lunch.

What happened? Jesus did not supply a free lunch. Instead, he challenged them about what they truly needed. Using the picture of his body (flesh) as bread and his blood, he challenged them to acknowledge that the only way for them to be saved was by eating his flesh and drinking his blood. What would this have meant to the crowd because Jesus was speaking before the Last Supper and the crucifixion? – Need to investigate this a bit more! (Note to self: If these people had been Africans, they would have thought that Jesus was a wizard or a member of some secret society

---

[2] Details about this commentary and other helpful resources are given in chapter 13 of this book.

(or cult). The more religious or spiritual among them would have suspected that he was possessed by a demon that was turning him into a cannibal, that is, a person who eats people's flesh and sucks their blood in the night. They would have begun a prayer of deliverance for him to cast out the demon. Can I use this idea somewhere in my sermon to help people understand things better? Or will it be a distraction?)

Who were the participants? The crowd were mainly Jews, although there may have been a few non-Jews there too (we know from chapter 4 in John and incidents recorded in the other gospels that there were some non-Jews who were interested in Jesus). These people are all called "disciples" in the passage because they were following Jesus around, but they were doing it for the wrong reasons (see above). They did not like it when Jesus confronted them with the truth about what they really needed. They weren't even prepared to do the work to try to understand his puzzling words about eating his body. They left as soon as they were challenged with hard truths. It seems that they may never even have been real disciples. They had no personal commitment to Jesus, but only wanted the things he could give them. They saw him as a source of food, rather than as a saviour. Peter's words show that the twelve disciples were committed to Jesus and to his teaching. That was why they stayed when the others left.

What was the effect? This incident made it clear who were real disciples and who were not.

Possible applications. What does this mean to us today? It is difficult to endure as a disciple of Jesus if we do not have a deep personal conviction about who Jesus is and what he does. If we are going to be true disciples we must accept him as both our Saviour and Lord. Peter's response reveals the need for conviction and commitment as requirements for anyone who wants to follow Jesus as his disciple.

Another possible application: the importance of getting our priorities straight. When I was reading this passage, I remembered the Old Testament story of Esau, who was more focused on food than on his birthright as the firstborn son of Isaac and Rebekah (Gen 25:29–34). The deserting disciples were like him in that they focused more on food than on Jesus as Saviour. Are we more focused on getting earthly things now, even if they do not last, than on eternal things that we will receive in the future?

Listen to What God Says to You

How can we hope to bring God's word to the people if we have not taken the time to hear what his word has to say to us? So as you read, study, ask questions and take notes, also take time to pray and reflect on what God is saying to you through this passage. How will you apply its truths in your life? You cannot honestly ask your hearers to do things that you yourself are unwilling to do.

9

PREPARING THE SERMON

There are different approaches to preparing or building sermons. Sometimes you will have spent much time studying a passage of Scripture and the theme of the sermon emerges from that study. At other times, you may have a topic you wish to preach on, and then spend time choosing the Bible passage from which to preach. Of course, the first way is good for an expository type of sermon while the second way is better for a topical type of sermon. But what both approaches have in common is that the preacher needs to have done a lot of work before actually sitting down to prepare the sermon as such. To continue with the building metaphor, we could say that the work of studying the passage or researching an idea is similar to a builder digging a good foundation. Now, as you start to prepare the sermon, you are starting to build the walls of the house.

Identify a Main Theme for the Sermon

When you begin your preparation and start studying the passage you plan to preach on, you probably have some idea of what you want to say in your sermon, but the idea is still very rough. Then as you read, reread and carefully study the passage, you will find that a main theme begins to emerge.

But it is also possible that as you read you identify several possible themes you could develop. Which one should you pursue? If you preach on all those themes in one sermon, your sermon may become too scattered and lose its impact. So once again you have to pray, asking

God to guide your thinking and give you wisdom as you choose what aspect of the passage to focus on. Then sit down, turn to a new page in the book in which you are taking your notes, and write down the question: *What is my purpose in preaching this sermon?*

Of course, the purpose of all preaching is to benefit the listener and bring glory and honour to God, but why are you planning to preach this particular sermon? What do you hope the sermon will achieve in your listeners? Be very specific in your answer and write it down before you begin to build your sermon.

That statement of purpose will function like the plumb line a builder hangs to make sure that the walls of a house are going up straight and not leaning to one side or the other. As you work on your sermon, keep returning to that answer and asking yourself, does this paragraph, this illustration, this application, fit in with the purpose of the sermon or is it a distraction from it? Are the walls of my sermon going up straight and strong, or are you wavering and dealing with too many issues at once?

Let us return to John 6:66–69, which I have been using as an example. What will be the theme of my sermon on that passage? As I have read and reread that passage, I have become aware of two themes I could preach on: "The reasons people follow Jesus" or "The requirements for being Jesus' disciple."

How do I decide which of these options to focus on? This is where my knowledge of the circumstances of the people I will be preaching to comes in. If I am preaching to a community where people are being attracted to the prosperity gospel, I may need to preach on the reasons why people follow Jesus, and challenge the congregation about their motives for following Jesus. Are they just looking for more bread? And what if the type of bread he offers is not the type of bread they want?

But suppose I am going to be preaching this sermon in a very poor community. The church members are so poor that they can barely pay the meagre allowance of the village evangelist. Now, an election is coming, and some corrupt politicians are trying to take advantage of the community's poverty and buy their votes. The church is divided on this matter. Some members see no problem in accepting the money; it will help them pay the evangelist's allowance and improve the church building. But other members think it is evil to sell their votes because this is dishonest and it goes against their Christian conscience to support a corrupt leader. In this context, my purpose in preaching this sermon is to encourage the members of the church in this poor community not to sell their principles.

So at the head of my page I write:

What is my purpose in preaching this sermon?

And then I summarize my thinking like this:

Purpose: *To encourage Christians in this poor community not to sell their principles.*

On the next line, I write,

What is the main point that I want to bring out in this sermon?

And then I summarize my thinking like this:

Main Point: *A true disciple of Jesus demonstrates personal conviction and commitment to him.*

This main point could be summarized still more in just one word:

Theme: *Commitment*

Prepare a Sermon Outline

Now I have dug a foundation and hung a plumb line. It is time to start building the walls by preparing a sermon outline. In Africa, evangelists and travelling preachers often preach without any form of written outline. They just preach the sermon idea that comes to mind. They are probably carrying on the African oral tradition in which information is not written down but is stored in memory. This tradition is also strong in the evangelism-oriented Christianity that was introduced to Africa by missionaries. An African evangelist does not need to have a formally structured outline in order to preach an evangelistic sermon.

However, you will find that a well-planned outline is very helpful when it comes to your regular preaching, where the goal is not only evangelism but also building up the church and teaching believers about their faith. A good outline is like the brick in the foundation of a house upon which the walls will rise. I could also compare it to a torch, which sends out a beam of light illuminating the path you are walking on, or to a car's headlights, which show you the good and bad parts of the road, the potholes to be avoided and the bend ahead where you can easily get onto the wrong road. In the same way a good sermon outline helps you to see where you are going with your sermon. It will help you avoid distractions by reminding you of the whole plan of the sermon, which is set out step-by-step from start to finish.

But a sermon outline is more than just a guide to be used when you are actually in the pulpit. It is also of great help as you prepare your sermon. It will help you plan the main points of the sermon and the subpoints which fall under each main point. We could think of the main points as the key stops on a journey. For example, it is possible to drive from Lagos in Nigeria to Accra in Ghana, but you can plan your trip better if you remember that you will be delayed at several international borders. There is the border between Nigeria and Benin, then the one between Benin and Togo, and then the border between Togo and Ghana. Only after going through that final border can you eventually reach Accra. In the same way, your sermon aims to lead people from your starting point to your conclusion. You can think of your main points as the border crossings in your sermon. The subpoints are more like checkpoints along the way. You need to go through them in order to reach your destination. By having these points marked on the map as you set out, you can avoid unpleasant surprises, and can judge that you are on the right route and will eventually reach your goal.

When you look at the outline for your sermon, you can see whether you have remembered to include all the key points. You become aware that you cannot go from Point 1 to Point 3 without passing through Point 2, just as you cannot go straight from Nigeria to Togo without going through Benin. If you omit Point 2, your hearers will not follow your argument. Or maybe you will see that you have put Point 2 in the wrong place, as if you were planning to go to Togo after going to Benin. So you need to rearrange the sermon so that the point is now in the right place.

Looking at your outline, you may also see that you have planned so many stops on the journey from your starting point to your conclusion that you cannot possibly hope to complete the journey in one day. So you may have to decide to split your sermon in two to avoid exhausting your listeners. You can preach the second half next Sunday. Or you may decide to cut out some interesting scenic detours and focus your sermon on only one or two points.

One sure way to know that your sermon is too long is to look at the number of main points and subpoints in your outline. If you see that you are going to be talking about Subpoint Seven of Point Three, you can be sure that your listeners will never remember that many points! Some of the points will need to go.

To sum up what I have been saying: An outline helps you as the preacher to see if all the parts of the sermon are appropriately connected to one another so that the listeners will not be confused when the sermon is preached.

Here is the outline I might use for a sermon on John 6:66–69.

Text: John 6:66–69

Purpose: To encourage Christians in this poor community not to sell their principles.

Main Point: A true disciple of Jesus demonstrates personal conviction and commitment.

Introduction: What is the difference between the two groups of people?

Main Point I: Why did some disciples leave Jesus? (vv. 66)

    Subpoint A: They rejected Jesus' teaching because it was difficult.

    Subpoint B: They left Jesus because he wouldn't do what they wanted.

Main Point II: Why did some disciples remain with Jesus? (vv. 67–69)

    Subpoint A: They were convinced that Jesus came from God.

    Subpoint B: They were committed to following him because

        Sub-subpoint 1. Jesus offers the hope of eternal life (v. 68)

        Sub-subpoint 2. Jesus is the Messiah, the one who brings us to God (v. 69)

Conclusion

If you want to see more examples of sermon outlines, and a few more tips on developing them, please turn to Appendix 1 at the back of the book.

Build the Sermon

Developing the outline of your sermon can also be compared to erecting the walls of your building. Once they are up, it is time to add the windows and the rafters. In other words, now that you have the structure of your sermon, it is time to add details.

What kind of details? Well, for example, you need to work out how to explain what each point in your sermon means. You may help the listeners think deeply about the passage by first asking questions (sometimes the same questions you asked yourself when studying the passage) before supplying the appropriate answers. For example, you could begin by asking why those who decide not to follow Jesus are called "disciples" in verse 66 – and then point out that not all those who claim to be disciples are truly disciples.

You also need to find good examples to illustrate the points you are making and so build a bridge from Jesus' day to the present. You do not want bad illustrations, which are like an awkward African drumbeat that is not in accord with a particular song and its dance step. A bad illustration will distract people from your message, whereas a good illustration will help them to understand it.

So what makes for a good illustration? A good illustration is one that is drawn from daily life (not one imported from some book of illustrations or collection of illustrations on the Web). It refers to something that people know, so that each time they see something related to the illustration, they remember your sermon. (Will you be reminded of my point about making the illustration dance with the rhythm of the sermon each time you hear a drum beat?)

A good illustration is also relevant to the sermon. It is not told just because you like telling stories about yourself or because it will make people laugh. Rather, the illustration sheds light on the point you are making and makes it easier for people to grasp. (Did my comparison of a sermon outline to car headlights help you to understand the point I was making?)

Finally, a good illustration connects well with the application you want to make. When I used the example of a car's headlights, I was making a point about seeing where you are going. The point and the illustration worked well together.

My next point may seem to contradict my earlier one, where I said that a good illustration is drawn from daily life. But it is closely related to the idea that the meaning of the Bible is found within the Bible itself, and to the fact that you want to show how separate parts of Scripture relate to the whole Bible. So sometimes we use other parts of the Bible to throw light on a passage we are studying. Thus your sermon outline may also include links to relevant passages of the Bible that support your point. By this I do not mean only quoting a long string of verses. Rather, I mean using a passage or a verse to throw light on the passage. For example, as you saw in my notes as I worked on this passage, I could include a reference to the story of Esau in Genesis 25. Esau was more focused on immediate food than on things that are of lasting value. In the same way, the people who left Jesus wanted only ordinary bread, not the Holy One of God.

Develop Your Application

Our goal in preaching is not only to help listeners get a better intellectual understanding of the teaching of the Bible. We also want to help them to know how what the Bible says applies to their daily life as citizens, farmers, fishermen, hunters, market women, students, house helps, office workers and businessmen. How do they live out what they believe as adults and youth, married and singles, husbands and wives, parents and children, leaders and followers, employers and employees? How does what they believe affect their relationships with their neighbours, and with anyone else they come in contact with.

Helping the listeners know how to apply what they have heard to their own lives is a very important step in building the sermon. This is called the application. An application will be most effective when a preacher has good knowledge of the background, lifestyle, culture and customs of the listeners, and the challenges they are presently experiencing. Crafting a good application is one of the important skills that a preacher needs to develop.

Do you remember the image of a plumb line that I used when speaking about the purpose of the sermon? Your application should be checked against that plumb line. Is the application you are planning to make directly linked to your purpose in preaching this sermon?

But no good builder will wait until the wall is completed before lowering the plumb line. It will be used at regular intervals to make sure the walls are still straight. And in the same way, you should not wait until the end of the sermon to make your application. If you leave all application till the end, your listeners may have forgotten about some point you were making earlier, and so the application will not be as strong in their minds. Or they may be thinking about what is going to happen after the service, and be eager to move on at the end of the sermon, and so may ignore your closing words. That is why it is a good idea to make applications in the course of your sermon. Apply the message as you explain each point. For example, in the sermon outlined above, you could challenge members about whether they will still follow Jesus if he does not immediately do what they want, or if what he says seems strange and difficult to accept. Are they like the unreliable disciples? You could make that application after Point I in the sermon, and then go on to talk about the nature of true disciples in Part II.

A good application should not come as a surprise. It should flow logically from the points of the sermon, and capture the main point of the sermon. It should challenge the listener to make a decision or take some action that is clearly related to the subject of the sermon.

Here is one example of a possible application that could be used in a sermon on John 6:66–69, which I have used as an example: "Following Jesus is not easy. It may involve following him when everyone else wants to go in a different direction. What gives us the strength to stay committed to him at such times? It is a deep personal conviction about who Jesus is and what he does. Peter must be our model. Like him, we must say that even if we don't fully understand everything that Jesus says, we will still follow him and accept his teaching because he is the one who has the words of life. So what about you? Is Jesus your Saviour and Lord? Will you follow him even when the crowd goes the other way?"

Pray

Your entire sermon preparation process should be bathed in prayer. As the time to preach approaches, you should pray for special protection against the attacks of the enemy and for good understanding on the part of the listeners.

It should not be forgotten that when you preach a sermon, you are only sowing the seed. It is God who waters it so that the message becomes meaningful to the individual listener and bears fruit in their lives. No preacher, no matter how eloquent, can change people's lives. Therefore, we need to ask God to cause changes in the listeners while the sermon is being preached. I have already told you how I used to pray over every pew in my church on a Saturday night, asking God to reveal himself to those who would sit there the next morning.

10

PREPARING YOUR INTRODUCTION AND CONCLUSION

You may be surprised that I am giving a whole chapter to the introduction and conclusion of your sermon. We tend to think of the body of the sermon as the meat of the meal, and the introduction and conclusion as of minor importance – they are just something we snack on while waiting for the meal to be ready. But that is not the case. The introduction is more like the invitation to the meal. If that is not done well, people will not come to the meal. They may sit in church, but they will not listen attentively to what you have to say. And the conclusion to a sermon is also extremely important. You are preaching the sermon for a purpose. You do not want to miss that purpose or leave your listeners confused about what you want them to do. So you need a strong conclusion to drive this point home.

The Introduction

You might have expected that we would talk about the introduction when we talked about the sermon outline. After all, the introduction comes before the main part of the sermon. But the decision to leave it till this point in the book was quite deliberate. Your introduction has to lead into the sermon, and how can you lead into something before you know what you are going to say? You need to have an outline before you know what you are introducing. There are many famous preachers who say that they leave the introduction till last when preparing a sermon!

The main purpose of an introduction is to encourage people to listen to what you will be saying. So you may want to capture their attention with a catchy story. But remember that not just any story will do. We do not want to spend our time telling tales by moonlight! Your story must be connected to your sermon in some way, so that when people remember the story, they also remember the sermon that followed it. In this way, your story can help boost their faith, not undermine it or distract them from it. We want them to be thinking about how they live and whether they are pleasing God, not about the wonderful life you are living.

Given that Africans love to sing, you may decide to use a song that is appropriate and relevant to the message as part of your introduction. When doing this, keep the song short. A few lines or at most one stanza will be enough to catch your hearer's attention.

Another way of starting a sermon is to ask a simple but relevant question: For example, thinking back to the notes I made when studying John 6:66–69, I might ask, "How would you react if someone came to you and told you to eat his flesh and drink his blood? Would you think he was bewitched, or that he was a witch himself?" Then you could lead into your sermon about how people responded when Jesus said this, and why they responded in different ways.

Or you could begin your sermon by referring to something that happened recently. For example, you might say, "I hear that a thief was caught in the village last night," and then go on to speak about how easily we can be separated from our earthly possessions, which is why it is foolish to walk away from the heavenly "bread" that Jesus offers.

Or you can begin by making some statement about how what you are going to be talking about applies to your listeners. We know that when someone speaks to the public, those listening want to know how what the speaker is talking about concerns them. Here is an example of such a statement, "I want to tell husbands in this congregation a secret no one has ever told you about how to make your wives love you more." Or you could say, "Sometimes, it can be harder to follow Jesus than to follow everyone else. Compromise can look very attractive."

You should always remember when preparing the introduction that its purpose is to get people to participate in the sermon by listening attentively to what you have to say from the Bible. This is why your introduction should be clearly linked to the theme of the sermon; short, appropriate to the sermon, and relevant to the life experience of the listeners.

After a good introduction, you can move on into the body of the sermon with ease and be assured of the people's attention.

The Conclusion

At the start of this chapter, we spoke about identifying the purpose of your sermon. We do not preach simply because we want people to listen to us; rather, we want them to listen to the word of God. His word always requires a clear and specific response. It is therefore very important to conclude every sermon well so that the listeners will know how to respond to it.

It is in the conclusion of the sermon that the main purpose and goal for preaching a particular sermon is clearly stated. You may have mentioned it before in the course of the sermon, but in the conclusion the main idea or truth of the sermon is driven home. At this point, every individual listener is made aware that the message in the sermon demands a personal response from him or her. Here, the preacher challenges the listeners to respond to the message directly and personally. It is at this time that the preacher inspires the listeners to act honestly on the message. The conclusion therefore helps to achieve the purpose of the sermon, acting as the "take home" for the listener.

There is an English saying, "If you don't know where you are going, how will you know that you have got there?" This applies to your sermon too. If you want your listeners to respond positively and appropriately to any sermon, you must be clear about the purpose or aim of the sermon from the time you start to prepare it. For example, is the sermon intended to change people's thinking or behaviour? Is it meant to encourage them in general or to motivate them to do something specific? Or is the sermon intended to issue a call for repentance and bring people to an encounter with God for salvation? Your answer to this question will help you decide how to conclude the sermon.

What are your options when it comes to concluding a sermon? You may want to end by summarizing the main ideas of your sermon. Or you could end with a targeted and purposeful prayer for healing, comfort, encouragement, protection, strength, confidence, wisdom, or success in life – whatever is relevant to the sermon you have just preached. You could choose to end a sermon with a song, hymn, or chorus that fits with your message and is relevant to the audience. Do not choose just any hymn or the focus of your message will be lost. It can also be a good idea to end with a question or questions that challenge listeners to reflect on the message and how it applies to their lives.

The traditional missionary type of ending for a sermon has been an invitation or "altar call". But if the nature of your sermon does not require such an invitation, do not extend one. People can respond to the preaching of the word of God in different ways, some of which we have already discussed above.

If you do choose to give an invitation, there are three types of invitations that can be used to end a sermon. The first is an open invitation to those who would like to come to faith in Christ. The second is given to those who are Christians but have backslidden into sin. This type of invitation is a call to repentance, restoration and rededication. Lastly, the listeners can be invited to offer themselves for Christian service through giving financially or even by going into fulltime service for the Lord.

Whatever form of conclusion you choose to use, you should plan it in advance so that it is clear, brief, personally directed to the listener, and to the point. It should not be vague and general, like, "God has spoken to all of us today and you should examine yourself and I will examine myself." Or, "This warning is for you and for me." No. When the sermon is about the sin of adultery, for example, the listener needs to be told precisely what should be done to correct the error or change the situation. Or, if a preacher preaches on God's hatred for rebellion and the effects of rebellion, the listener needs to know how to respond to his own rebellious thoughts and to rebellion in others.

If a sermon ends in such a way that the listeners do not know exactly what to do about the message, the conclusion is confusing and weak. Preach and conclude the sermon in such a manner that the listeners are not only gripped and "cut to the heart" but are also left in no doubt about what they are to do in response.

11

PREACHING YOUR SERMON

Preaching, and Bible-centred preaching in particular, requires interaction between the preacher and the audience. We must never forget that preaching is about communicating a message. Therefore we need to master good communication skills if we are to be effective preachers whose message is heard and understood. This is another reason why it is very important to know the people to whom we are preaching. The better we know them the better we will be able to interact with them as we preach. Blending traditional African ways with modern ways of speaking to the public will greatly enhance our effectiveness when we stand in the pulpit to present the word of God.

Begin Well

At the start of any meeting in an African community, the most senior elder, who chairs the meeting, welcomes all those who are present and explains the purpose of the gathering. This is a good way to start the business of the day.

We should not forget these courtesies when we stand up to preach. We should take care to let the audience or listeners know that they are important. Stand in the pulpit with a smile, and greet the congregation properly. If you are a visiting preacher, it does no harm to quote something good that you have been told about the congregation, such as "Mr. Kofi told me that the people living here treat every visitor well. That has certainly been my experience. Thank you so much for your welcome to me."

If you are rude to the congregation and ignore them or act as if you are the only important person present, you will have lost your audience before you even begin your sermon.

Only after you have greeted the congregation should you launch into the introduction to your sermon, which should be so good that the audience will know without your telling them that this is not a sermon that was drafted as you walked into the church, but is an important message that you have spent much time preparing. That time spent in preparation is also a sign of respect and politeness to your congregation. You are not offering them your leftovers but your best work. It is not only God whom we honour when we prepare well.

Build Rapport with Your Audience

Have you ever been involved in a conversation in which the person you were talking to kept looking sideways at a television screen? Or have you ever tried to talk to someone who would not look at you but kept scanning the crowd, as if looking for someone more interesting to talk to? We know how annoying conversations like this are. But do you have the same sort of conversations when you are preaching? There are some pastors who are so nervous when they stand up that they cannot look at the congregation. Instead, they look at the ceiling, or at their notes, or out the window.

It is very important that you look at the people you are preaching to. Not only does this help them to relate to you, but it gives you important clues about how your message is being heard. Does everyone look bored? Is this a sign that you have been talking too long, or that they do not understand you? Do you need to adjust your sermon? Or as you look around, do you see some people in the congregation listening intently, or even nodding their heads in agreement with what you say? That is a good indication that they are understanding what is being said.

Making contact with the audience does not only involve using your eyes. It also involves thinking about the words you use. There are some preachers who like to use words to impress people. They favour academic vocabulary and use words like "exegesis" and "dichotomy" and "parousia" that no one in the congregation understands. They are like the Nigerian pastor who used so many impressive words in his preaching that his church members nicknamed him Wole "Shoyinka".[1] We should not be preaching to impress people; our goal should be to clearly express the mind of the God of the Bible to them. It is therefore very important to speak at the level of the audience, using simple words and expressions that are familiar to them, as well as familiar proverbs.

Use Good Communication Techniques

There was once a seminary student who was sure he would be a great preacher and who eagerly accepted opportunities to preach. So he was thrilled when he was asked to preach on a Christian television programme. On the day that the half-hour programme aired, he went to his pastor's house, arriving early so that he could watch the programme with the pastor. As his face appeared on the television, his heart swelled with pride. But as the pastor listened to the sermon, the student heard him say, "eh-eh-eh-eh-eh." Clearly something was not right. The problem was that the student had not bothered to learn anything about good communication techniques. He enjoyed preaching, but his audience did not enjoy listening. Most of them would have turned off the television.

The student thought that he was preaching very well and expected praise from his pastor. But that was not the case. Instead, he was advised to avoid talking non-stop, almost without pausing to take a breath, and to learn how to pace his message better.

If you do not want to be like that young man, and do want to be a really effective speaker, you need to learn some basic communication techniques. These include learning how to use your voice appropriately. Do not speak too softly or too loudly – few people enjoy being shouted at. Instead, aim to achieve a volume that people are comfortable with. Try to be aware of the pace at which you speak. If you speak too fast, people will miss what you are saying. But if you speak too slowly, they will become bored. And if you speak in the same way all the time, that too is boring to listeners. You need to learn to use your voice like a

---

[1] A pun on the name of the Nobel Prize winning writer Wole Soyinka.

musical instrument, raising it when appropriate, and lowering it at other times.

The next point may seem too obvious to mention, but it is still important. When you speak with your friends, you may speak in any style you want, but when you speak in a public place, you need to use good grammar and correct vocabulary. If you want to quote proverbs, make sure that you are quoting them correctly and using them in an appropriate context. This applies to whatever language you are speaking. You will find that people will judge the acceptability of your message by the acceptability of the language in which it is preached.

Finally, remember that when you preach it is not only your voice that communicates; your whole body helps to convey your message. Does the way you stand indicate that you are excited about what you are saying, or suggest that you are bored by your own sermon? Does your posture match what you are talking about? For example, if you are preaching from Acts 1:10 where it says that the disciples looked up as Jesus was taken into heaven, you too should look up, and not down.

Remember that your hands are also part of your body, and the way you use them also communicates. If you are nervous and fidget with your hands, your hearers will be distracted. So try to be aware of how you are using your hands, and what gestures you make with them. Even a standard gesture can become distracting if it is used too often.

Help Your Audience Follow the Flow of Your Sermon

An African proverb says, "When the drumbeat changes, the dance step will also change." African dancers listen for a change in the drumbeat and adapt their dance appropriately each time the rhythm changes. Every dance step has to be in keeping with the particular drumbeat.

The same applies to preaching the Bible. Just as a good drummer knows how to adjust the pace and signal changes that inspire and excite the dancers, so you need to know how to adjust the pace and signal the changes in your sermon as you move from one point to the next.

The act of moving from one part of the sermon to the next is called making a transition, and the words used as the preacher moves from one point to the next are called connectors. These are phrases or statements that signal to the listeners that the preacher is moving on to the next point. Sometimes these connectors are just one word, like "therefore" or "but". But if you use only one-word connectors, you will find that some of your hearers miss that word, and then they get lost. Their minds are continuing down the old track, while your sermon has switched to a new track. So sometimes it is better to make the connectors stand out by using an entire sentence or phrase. For example, if you were preaching on our example passage, you could ask a question like "Why did the people follow Jesus in the first place?" and pause for a moment to allow people to think about the answer to that question. Then later you can tell people where you have been and where you are going by saying, "We have looked at some bad reasons for following Jesus; now let us look at some good reasons for following him." We can also introduce explanations by saying, "We have learnt about … Now let us see what its practical effects are." And you can summarize what you have been saying: "I have told you that the first reason for … is …, and that the second reason is … The last one is …"

When the right connectors are used, your listeners will be able to follow the logical flow of your sermon. If you are watching their faces, you will be able to tell that this is the case, and may even see some of them nodding in agreement with you.

Be Honest about What the Bible Says

A growing number of preachers say and do unbelievable things in the name of God, while falsely claiming that the Bible supports them. Sometimes they will even quote Bible verses taken out of context so that their meaning is twisted. This is an abusive way of using the Bible in preaching. Such a preacher is lying about what God or the Bible says.

Here is an example of what I am speaking of. Years ago, a Nigerian pastor used Ephesians 5:23–24 to justify his immoral behaviour. He preached, "The Bible says Christ is the head of the church, which means that I as the pastor am the neck of the church, and you members are the body. The head does not communicate directly to the body but to the neck, and the neck then communicates his message to the body. The message he has communicated to me is that I must divorce my wife and marry another [a women who was a member of the church]. My wife is not allowed to complain about this, because the Bible also says that wives are to submit to their husbands in everything."

Do you see where he went wrong? Nowhere in the Bible are pastors called the neck of the church. There is also no mention of divorce in that passage in Ephesians. It also does not say that wives are to submit to what is ungodly and dishonouring to God. The pastor was avoiding the truth that both he and the congregation are supposed to be under the authority of Christ, the owner of the church.

When you preach, you must seek to remain true to the Scriptures. You must lead the reader or listener into the Bible through good interpretation, clear explanation, and relevant application. The congregation must be able to open their own Bibles and follow your argument in the sermon.

Note that being honest also means admitting that sometimes you do not understand everything that the Bible says. There is no shame in that. After all, even Peter and the other disciples were puzzled about what Jesus meant when he spoke about eating his body. So you need to be prepared to admit that you sometimes find some passages puzzling and have had to work hard to understand them. Your listeners will be blessed by your honesty and by the example you set them of diligent study of God's word.

12

SUMMARY AND SAMPLE SERMON

Summary

Let me summarize the step-by-step process for preparing a sermon we have outlined so far.

1. Pray for insight and wisdom as you prepare and for good understanding and definite action on the part of the listeners.
2. Read the chosen passage from the Bible several times and in different translations.
3. Ask relevant questions that can lead to good information that helps to build the sermon.
4. Take notes while you read and note down any answers you find to the questions you asked.
5. Choose an appropriate topic for the sermon.
6. Create the sermon outline.
7. Using the outline, build the sermon by developing each point with explanations, illustrations, questions and supporting Scriptures, and be sure to include the application.

We have looked at all the steps listed above except the last. It is now time to practically demonstrate how to build a sermon using the outline from John 6:66–69 that we developed earlier.

Record Keeping

However, before we look at the sermon, there is one other useful point of advice that I want to give you: *Keep a record of the sermons you preach*. As you look at the sermon below, you will see that the first item on the page records the name of the preacher, the text preached on, the title of the sermon, and details of where it was preached. This is useful information for your own records. If you keep these sermons filed by the verses you preached on, you can avoid making the mistake of preaching the same sermon, or a very similar sermon, twice in the same church. That is a good reason to record some details of the contents of the sermon too. You do not want to use exactly the same illustration too often.

Another possible reason for keeping a record of your sermons is for historical purposes. In the future, someone may want to study what was preached in this era or to compare the preaching style of preachers in Nigeria, or Kenya, or elsewhere in Africa. Your records of the sermons you preached may be very useful for such research.

Now, let us look at one possible sermon on John 6:66–69. In this case, I have made up the name of a preacher – we can call him Rev. Chukuemeka Kofi Mutunga – and I have made up the name of the church.

Sample Sermon

Sermon Preached by Rev. Chukuemeka Kofi Mutunga at the Redeemed Community Worship Centre of Dong, Plateau State, Nigeria on Sunday 13 May 2013 at 9:00 am

Text: John 6:66–69
Purpose: *To encourage Christians in this poor community not to sell their principles.*
Theme: *A true disciple of Jesus demonstrates personal conviction and commitment.*

Introduction

People who look similar can actually be very different. Think about the farmers in your village. Some of them work very hard on their farms, while others do very little. What makes the difference? Is it their attitude to their farm? Is it the value they attach to the farm?

Think too about Christians you know. Lots of people come to church, but why is it that some of them are determined to follow Jesus, while others turn to African Traditional Religion, or just stop following Jesus as soon as things get difficult? What makes the difference?

John's Gospel gives us one answer to the question, because the same problem existed in Jesus' day as you will see when we read John 6:66–69. Let's read that passage together now, while thinking about my question: What is the difference between the people who keep following Jesus and those who stop following him.

I. Why Did Some Disciples Leave Jesus? (v. 66)

Many people who had been acting as if they were disciples of Jesus suddenly "turned back and no longer followed him" (v. 66). Why would they do this? As the African proverb says, "Water does not taste sour without a cause." Let's look at what happened to cause them to leave.

Jesus had just been preaching about who he was, where he came from, and what he could give to those who placed true personal faith in him. He had been saying things like "I am the bread of life" (v. 35). He was proclaiming his unique relationship with God and saying that "everyone who has heard the Father and learned from him comes to me" (v. 46). He promised those who came to him eternal life: "Very truly I tell you, the one who believes in me has eternal life" (v. 47).

Then he used the picture of bread and blood to say that those who reject him do not become the children of God. To become God's children, they need to eat Jesus' flesh and drink his blood (v. 53). In other words, he was teaching that the only qualifying ticket for anyone to enter the kingdom was to believe in him and accept him as the Messiah the prophets had talked about. He was even more life-giving than the miraculous manna that had fed the Israelites when they were in the desert.

Some people had been happy to follow Jesus around while he was just being kind and healing people and telling good stories. But now he was making some very specific claims about what they needed to believe. That was when they started arguing with him. They were horrified at the idea of eating his flesh and drinking his blood – just as we would be if we heard someone say this! But they didn't take time to find out what he meant when he said this. They did not ask him for an explanation. They were not ready to seek the truth. Instead, they left him and went back to what they were doing before they followed him.

These people rejected Jesus as soon as his teaching became difficult.

But there was also another reason why they left him: *Jesus would not do what they wanted.*

We can see if we look back to what happened at the start of John 6, before he began teaching them. Just the day before, Jesus had given 5000 people a miraculous meal. Some of those people had hurried after Jesus, and settled down to listen to him again (vv. 24–25). They were happy to hear him preach if they could look forward to good food at the end of the service! (does that sound at all familiar?) But they really had no interest in the spiritual food he had to offer.

Jesus made it clear that he was well aware of their attitude:

> Jesus answered, "Very truly I tell you, you are looking for me, not because you saw the signs I performed but because you ate the loaves and had your fill." (v. 26)

Jesus then made it clear that he was not going to do what they wanted.

"Do not work for food that spoils, but for food that endures
to eternal life, which the Son of Man will give you. For on him
God the Father has placed his seal of approval." (v. 27)

The people were disappointed, but they decided to settle for something
else. So they asked Jesus what "works" God wanted them to do. They
probably expected him to say something like "keep the Sabbath, pray
five times a day, and be kind to your neighbours". Their focus was on
how to live in this world.

Once again, Jesus refused to do what they wanted. His response
to their question about "works" pointed not to earthly things but to
spiritual ones: "The work of God is this: to believe in the one he has
sent" (v. 29).

But the so-called "disciples" who were focused on bread and this
world weren't interested in accepting Jesus as the Son of God and the
one whom God had sent to save the world. Their focus on this life
stopped them from accepting his teaching about eternal life.

However, they hid their rejection of him behind a request for him to
perform some miraculous sign that would convince them that he came
from God. Not surprisingly, given that they had followed him because
they wanted more bread, they asked him to duplicate what Moses had
done when he provided manna in the wilderness. That was why they
asked for "bread from heaven" (v. 31). In other words, they wanted a
sign that would benefit them and give them food to eat.

Not surprisingly, Jesus refused and told them that he himself was
the bread that came from above; and that anyone who believed in him
would have their hunger satisfied and their thirst quenched (v. 35). More
than that, he insisted that this spiritual bread was far superior to merely
material bread. The people who had eaten the bread Moses supplied
had all died, but those who fed on Jesus would have eternal life (v. 40).

The people refused to listen to what Jesus was saying. They kept
their focus on this world, and said "we know your parents – so you can't
have come from God" (v. 42). They did not bother to ask for any more
explanation, or wait to learn more before deciding what to do, or think
about heavenly things, they simply walked away from Jesus because he
would not do what they wanted.

What about you? Are you frustrated because God is not giving you the things you want – marriage and children, a better house, better clothes, better food, a car or a bicycle? Are you focusing only on these material things, and forgetting about the spiritual blessings Jesus gives and the hope of eternal life?

Or are you puzzled about some things Jesus said? If so, you are not alone. But is that a good reason to walk away from him and abandon the hope of eternal life? We see that these disciples who left Jesus walked away from him and out of the pages of history. There were other disciples who were also puzzled, but who decided to stay. And we know what happened to them because we read about them in the gospels and Acts. But what made the difference? Why did these disciples decide to stay?

II. Why Did Some Disciples Remain with Jesus? (v. 68)

The disciples who stayed with Jesus would probably agree with those who left that what Jesus had said was "a hard teaching" (v. 60). But *they stayed because they had convictions about Jesus.*

Let me define what I mean here by convictions. We sometimes speak of someone being "convicted" when they are found guilty of doing something illegal. What the words mean in that context is that the judge is fully convinced that they are guilty of the crime. But we also have personal convictions – things that we believe very strongly. For example, when one of our daughters was in nursery school, she used to sing the songs they were taught in school. Sometimes, she got the words wrong, but she would not accept any correction from her mother. She insisted that she was singing what her teacher had taught them, and that her mother was wrong. Our daughter believed her teacher rather than her mother because she was convinced her "Aunty" could not be wrong about anything.

Can you see what conviction is? It is a strong belief that is not easily changed. The first group of disciples walked away from Jesus simply because they lacked conviction that he was the Son of God and the Messiah whom the Jews were expecting. Their belief in him was shallow rather than deep-seated.

By contrast, *the faithful disciples were both convinced that Jesus came from God and committed to following Jesus.*

Commitment is a sign of someone's complete devotion or dedication to someone, to a relationship, or to something that he or she decides to do. When a person is committed to something, we will see them put all their strength, time, energy, loyalty, and personal resources into that cause, or person. They will not give up when things get difficult. The life of the late evangelist Paul Gindiri from Nigeria is a good example of what it means to be committed to following Jesus.

Paul Gindiri, who was one of the leaders of the New Life for All evangelistic group, was very zealous and committed to preaching the gospel, especially to Muslims in Jos and in northern Nigeria. But he was also a businessman and the owner of a very successful stone-crushing company. He used the revenue from this company to care for his family, but also made large contributions to New Life for All and used his own money and vehicles to transport those who travelled with him on evangelistic journeys. He refused to stop preaching, even when his preaching led to threats against his life and his business. He was a man who pledged unflinching loyalty to Christ and sacrificed his life, time, strength, and resources in service to him.[1]

Following Jesus as his true disciples means more than words. It is showing that one has faith in him by what one does. True disciples have such strong *convictions* about who Jesus is that they live out their *commitment* to him, and refuse to give it up. Not even poverty or suffering can change their position.

What about you? Are you committed to following Jesus in all that you do and think? Or are you more like the other group, the people who were only interested in the benefits they could get from Jesus, and were not prepared to see their lives transformed? When we allow bad situations in life to determine our decisions and actions, we are no different from the people who looked for Jesus only for food and not for the truth that sets people free.

But what was it that the disciples who remained with Jesus believed that gave them such strong convictions and commitment? We know the answer to that question because of Peter's reply to Jesus' question, "You

---

[1] For more information on this evangelist, see Gyang Luke Dung, *Paul G. Gindiri: The Firebrand Evangelist* (Jos, Nigeria: Gyang Luke Dung, 2002).

do not want to leave too, do you?" (John 6:67). They were confronted with a choice – would they walk away or remain with Jesus?

Peter's response to the crucial question was, "Lord, to whom shall we go? You have the words of eternal life. We have come to believe and know that you are the Holy One of God" (John 6:68–69). That was why they were determined to stay with Jesus – that much is clear. But what do phrases like "the words of eternal life" actually mean?

When Peter speaks of Jesus' "words", he is referring to all of Jesus' teaching. As he spent time with Jesus, *Peter had become convinced that Jesus was indeed speaking "the words of eternal life"* when he said that all those who place personal faith in him will live with him in eternity after life on earth is ended. This is the truth that Jesus would restate when he said, "I am the way and the truth and the life. No one comes to the Father except through me" (John 14:6).

Peter had also become convinced that Jesus was telling the truth when he spoke about his relationship with God, and that he was indeed "the Holy One of God". This title for Jesus is similar to Peter's words when Jesus asked, "Who do you say I am" and Peter replied, "You are the Christ, the Son of the living God" (Matt 16:16). Peter is saying that Jesus really is "the Christ" – that is, the Messiah or Saviour the Jews were anticipating to come and save them from the political and economic oppression of the Romans. But Peter is beginning to see that Jesus is much more than a political Messiah; he now sees Jesus primarily as a spiritual deliverer – "the Holy One of God".

Because of these *convictions*, Peter and the rest of the Twelve were *committed* to following Christ. They believed in him and accepted his authority over them as their master. They had knowingly and willingly chosen to follow him, live with him, and to serve him. They knew that no other teacher or political leader could give them what Jesus had given them – eternal life. That is why they chose to stay with him even when Jesus offered them the opportunity to leave by asking whether they also wanted to go away with those who were confused by and rejected his teaching.

This is true commitment to the truth of his teaching and to the reality of his person. Without true personal commitment to Jesus as Lord and without total loyalty to him, it is difficult to remain in and with him when we face perplexing situations and do not understand what he is doing. But true commitment to Christ helps us to make the right decision. It will keep us from selling our Christian principles and betraying our conscience just so we can have some of our material needs supplied. When we place our convictions and commitment to him above all else, it will also be said of us someday as it was said of those saints who have gone before us, "Therefore God is not ashamed to be called their God" (Heb 11:16b).

Conclusion

Have people sometimes promised to do something or give certain things in the past, but failed to fulfil their promises? We all know that people have failed us, and that we have sometimes failed them too.

But what about Jesus? The deserting disciples left Jesus because he was failing to give them bread. They were willing to vote for him (or be his supporters) if he gave them the kind of bread they wanted. Jesus could have used this opportunity to increase his fame or popularity. After all, earlier on, the same group had wanted to make him king (v. 15)! But unlike some politicians today, Jesus did not want supporters who had no deep conviction and real commitment to him and his teaching. So he refused to give them bread.

But had Jesus ever promised to give these people bread? No, he had never promised to give them the sort of bread they were looking for. Instead, what he promised to give them was eternal life, and he does not fail on this promise. Human beings can and have failed. But it is not possible for Jesus to fail. This chorus puts it well:

> Jesus is the Rock, the solid Rock;
> Jesus is the solid Rock.
> I have found in him a resting place;
> Jesus is the solid Rock.

I invite you to look only to him and put your trust in him alone in your life, family, farming work, business, and fishing. Let us stand strong in our faith against every temptation and say like Peter, "Lord, to whom shall we go?" Then we shall sing another chorus:

> I have decided to follow Jesus;
> I have decided to follow Jesus.
> I have decided to follow Jesus;
> No turning back, no turning back.

This chorus expresses faith, deep trust, and true loyalty to Jesus. Only true and serious Christians can sing it honestly and truthfully. If we, as members of the Redeemed Community Worship Centre, are truly Christ's disciples, let us keep our conviction and remain faithful and committed to him even in our poverty. We should not be like the crowd who were willing to sell their votes to anyone who fed them, yet were not willing to accept Jesus' teaching and his offer of free eternal life. Let us, instead, be like the small group of disciples that remained with Jesus.

What I have presented above is one sample sermon in which I have tried to apply the principles outlined in this book. Read it through again, noting how I have woven the main points I identified in my outline, the text of Scripture, illustrations, and applications into the cloth of the sermon. Note too that this sermon does not only deal with spiritual life, but also with issues of day-to-day life. It will challenge non-believers, lukewarm believers and committed believers!

Another sample sermon is given in Appendix 2. You might want to read that sermon carefully too, seeing how it too incorporates the principles we have been studying.

13

CONCLUSION

In some parts of Africa, there are more farmers than there are office workers. Whether they are growing yams, cassava, cocoyam, rice, corn, or bananas, these farmers know the importance of taking care of the crop from the time it is sown to the time it is harvested. They keep their farms free of weeds and protect the growing crop from raiding monkeys, straying domestic animals, and the herds of nomadic farmers. They also do what is needed to provide nutrients for the crop and to fight off attacks by insect pests and rodents.

Preachers and teachers of the Bible in modern Africa are like these farmers in that they too are cultivating a crop that needs careful tending and protection from spiritual attacks and distractions. If they want to grow a godly congregation, they need to work hard to preach the types of sermons that will have positive effects and boost the spiritual growth of the listeners.

As Christians grow to healthy maturity, hearing biblical messages that are relevantly applied to their life situations, the church will become stronger and the gospel will have a more powerful influence on our communities. After all, the Scriptures are given to transform and to guide people. The purpose of preaching the Scriptures is to bring people to Christ and to affect the way Christians live as witnesses for Christ and how they serve God in their communities. Godly believers will improve the quality of Christian life and witness in Africa.

When the biblical message is correctly and appropriately communicated, it will change people's lives and attitudes. The challenge we face as preachers is our willingness and ability to learn how to fulfil the charge Paul gave to Timothy: "Present yourself to God as one approved, a workman who does not need to be ashamed and who correctly handles the word of truth" (2 Tim 2:15). Preachers have a responsibility to work hard to study the Bible carefully and honestly. When they do this, they will also be able to preach the word; be prepared in season and out of season; correct, rebuke and encourage – with great patience and careful instruction" (2 Tim 4:2).

It is hoped that this book will help you as you work to cultivate the attitude of careful study of the Scriptures and develop the skill of simple but clear presentation of the message of the Scriptures.

14

RESOURCES TO HELP YOU GROW AS A PREACHER

As preachers, it can be helpful to have books that help us understand the Bible and preach it better. There are many such books available, but some of the books listed below are particularly helpful because they were written by African scholars for African pastors, or were written by Western scholars with a deep desire to serve pastors in areas that lack other resources.

Books to Help You Study the Bible

Tokunboh Adeyemo (ed.), *Africa Bible Commentary*. Jos and Nairobi: Hippo/Grand Rapids: Zondervan, 2006.

The first one-volume Bible commentary produced in Africa by African theologians to meet the needs of African pastors, students, and lay leaders. Interpreting and applying the Bible in the light of African culture and realities, it furnishes powerful and relevant insights into the biblical text that transcend Africa in their significance. The *Africa Bible Commentary* gives a section-by-section interpretation that provides a contextual, readable, affordable, and immensely useful guide to the entire Bible. It also includes more than seventy special articles dealing with topics of key importance for ministry in Africa and around the world. This commentary is currently available in English, French, Portuguese, Swahili and Malagasy, and work is underway on translations into Hausa and Amharic.

Africa Study Bible. Carol Stream: Tyndale, 2017.

Based on the New Living Translation, this Study Bible includes brief introductions to each book of the Bible, application points, and many links to African proverbs and stories.

Michael Eaton, *The Branch Commentary*. Carlisle: Langham Preaching Resources, 2019.

Over the course of his career as a pastor, Michael Eaton did his utmost to preach on the whole Bible. This commentary gathers those sermons and publishes them in a form that will be helpful to preachers and Bible readers. The style is lively and engaging, but there is also great spiritual depth.

Africa Bible Commentary Series. Jos and Nairobi: Hippo/Grand Rapids: Zondervan.

All the books in this series of commentaries on individual books of the Bible are written by African scholars. Each commentary is divided into preachable units and written for preachers. Extensive endnotes dealing with more academic issues make these books useful for students too. To date, the following works have been published:

Bungishabaku Katho *Jeremiah and Lamentations* (currently only available in French, but in the process of being translated into English)

Solomon Andria *Romans* (also available in French)

Samuel Ngewa *Galatians*

Samuel Ngewa *1 & 2 Timothy and Titus*

Books about Preaching and Bible Interpretation

Femi Adeleye, *Preachers of a Different Gospel*. Jos and Nairobi: Hippo/Grand Rapids: Zondervan, 2011.

"Name it and claim it!" "Just have faith!" "Give and you will get!" Catchphrases like this have convinced many Christians that trusting in God will bring health and wealth. But the gospel does not promise prosperity without pain or salvation without sanctification. Femi Adeleye draws on his wide-ranging experience as he examines the appeal and peril of this new gospel of prosperity that has made deep inroads in Africa, as well as in the West.

Michael Kyomya, *A Guide to Interpreting Scripture: Context, Harmony, and Application*. Jos and Nairobi: Hippo/Grand Rapids: Zondervan, 2010.

Misconceptions about what the Bible actually says can breed confusion and false ideas about God and our Christian life. So it is important that we interpret it carefully. Ugandan Bishop Michael Kyomya explains what interpretation is, why it is important, how to do it, and what pitfalls to avoid. He illustrates his points with examples from his own experience and from sermons he has heard in Africa. His presentation makes it clear that interpretation is not just something for scholars, but is useful when preparing a sermon or a Sunday school lesson, and in our own personal study of the Bible. The writing is simple and clear, and the illustrations are both amusing and informative.

Conrad Mbewe, *Pastoral Preaching*. Carlisle: Langham Preaching Resources, 2017.

A practical guide to preaching by a Zambian preacher who has been acclaimed as the African Spurgeon. The focus is not only on preaching that will nurture a congregation but also on the character and spiritual nurture of the preacher.

Mark Meynell, *What Angels Long to Read: Reading and Preaching the New Testament*. Carlisle: Langham Preaching Resources, 2017.

An introduction to the New Testament combined with practical guidelines on how to go about preaching from the gospels, the letters, and Revelation. This book is a companion to Chris Wright's book, *Sweeter than Honey*.

Christopher J. H. Wright, *Sweeter than Honey: Preaching the Old Testament*. Carlisle: Langham Preaching Resources, 2015.

Many preachers ignore preaching from the Old Testament because they feel it is outdated in light of the New Testament and difficult to expound. On the other hand some preachers will preach from the Old Testament frequently but fail to "handle" it correctly, turning it into moralistic rules or symbolic lessons for our spiritual life. In this book, Christopher J. H. Wright proclaims that preachers must not ignore the Old Testament. It is the word of God! The Old Testament lays the foundation for our faith and it was the Bible that Jesus read and used. Looking first at why we should preach from the Old Testament, the author moves on to show the reader how they can preach from it. Covering the History, Law, Prophets, Psalms and Wisdom Literature, interspersed with practical checklists, exercises and sermons, the reader is provided with an essential guide on how to handle from the Old Testament correctly.

John Piper, *The Supremacy of God in Preaching.* Grand Rapids: Baker, 2015.

A classic resource that stresses the importance of proclaiming the word of God when we preach. It highlights three main aspects of preaching: the goal of preaching is the glory of God; the ground of preaching is the cross of Christ; and the gift of preaching is the power of the Holy Spirit.

John Stott, *The Challenge of Preaching.* Carlisle: Langham Preaching Resources, 2013/Grand Rapids: Eerdmans, 2015.

Internationally esteemed as an expository preacher and evangelical spokesman, John Stott edified thousands of Christian preachers and listeners during his lifetime. This book abridges and revises the text of Stott's *Between Two Worlds: The Challenge of Preaching Today,* first published in 1982, and updates it for our twenty-first-century context. Through Greg Scharf's abridging and updating work, John Stott's perspectives and insights on faithful, relevant preaching of the word of God will benefit a new generation of preachers and preachers-to-be.

APPENDIX 1

EXAMPLES OF SERMON OUTLINES

The outlines presented below represent a few of the many sermons I have had the opportunity to preach. They are offered here to anyone who would find them helpful.

The outlines are arranged in the same order as the Bible passages on which they are based. Each lists the main points of the sermon and the subpoints which fall under each main point. Sometimes the subpoints are also broken down into smaller points which I call sub-subpoints. When numbering the parts of the outline, the main points are given Roman numerals (I, II, etc.) while the subpoints are usually given letters (A, B, etc.). As a rule then, when an outline has I, there must be II; when it has an A, there must also be B; and where there is number 1, there also must be number 2.

If, for instance, you are preaching a sermon that has two main points, and the first main point has two subpoints, the second has three subpoints and the last subpoint is further broken down into two sub-subpoints, your numbering would look like this:

I. Main Point
   A. Subpoint
   B. Subpoint
II. Main Point
   A. Subpoint
   B. Subpoint
   C. Subpoint
      1. Sub-sub point
      2. Sub-sub point

The sermons outlined below were preached to different congregations, on different occasions, and for different purposes. However, I have not included this background information because my purpose is simply to illustrate how to create a sermon outline.

I make no claim that these are the best, or even the only, outlines that could be used when preaching on these passages. My sole aim in presenting them is to help you see how to outline a sermon and come to appreciate how creating an outline allows for a free flow of thought and ease of presentation.

SERMON OUTLINE 1

Text: *Deuteronomy 6:10–19*
Topic: *Have you forgotten the Lord?*
Purpose: *To remind Christians not to become complacent in times of prosperity.*
Introduction

I.   Why we need to be reminded to remember the Lord, vv. 10–12

    A.   Prosperity offers many distractions, vv. 10–11

    B.   It is easy to forget the source of our prosperity, v. 12

II.   How we are to remember the Lord, vv. 13–19

    A.   By remaining committed to God, vv. 13–16

    B.   By consistently doing what is right, vv. 17–19

Conclusion

SERMON OUTLINE 2

Text: *Psalm 54*
Topic: *A prayer of confidence*
Purpose: *To encourage Christians to trust God and depend on him like David did.*
Introduction

I.   David expressed confidence in God when he prayed for salvation, vv. 1–4

II.   David expressed confidence in God's justice when he prayed for the punishment of the wicked, v. 5

III.   David expressed confidence in God's deliverance when he planned to offer sacrifice to him, vv. 6–7

Conclusion

SERMON OUTLINE 3

Text: *Acts 4:32–37(see also 2:42–47)*
Topic: *The caring community*
Purpose: *To encourage Christians to cultivate a positive community life*
Introduction
I. The basis for the disciples' welfare scheme, vv. 32–33
   A. They kept Jesus' command to be one, v. 32; John 17:20–23
   B. They kept Jesus' command to love one another, v. 33; John 13:33–34
II. The way in which they served the needy, vv. 34–37
   A. They had a common purse for the needy, v. 34
   B. They gave to the needy as the need arose, v. 35
Conclusion

SERMON OUTLINE 4

Text: *Philippians 2:5–11*
Topic: *Imitate Christ's attitude of humility*
Purpose: *To motivate Christians to live like Christ did*
Introduction
I. How Christ showed his humility, vv. 5–8
   A. He was willing to relinquish his rights, vv. 5–7
   B. He was willing to stoop down to achieve God's purpose, v. 8
II. The reward for Christ's humility, vv. 9–11
   A. He has been exalted to the highest place, v. 9
   B. He is to be revered by all, vv. 10–11
Conclusion

SERMON OUTLINE 5

Text: *1 Thessalonians 4:13–18; see John 14:1–3*
Topic: *Holding on to hope*
Purpose: *To comfort grieving Christians*
I. Reasons for hope
   A. Jesus Christ died and rose again, v. 14
   B. Jesus Christ will return, v. 16
II. What we hope for
   A. Reunion with believers who have died, vv. 13–15

    B. Being with Christ forever, v. 17

III. The result of our hope

    A. Comfort, v. 13

    B. Confidence, v. 18

Conclusion

SERMON OUTLINE 6

Text: *Revelation 2:12–17*

Topic: *Persevering to win the prize*

Purpose: *To encourage Christians in hostile environments to remain faithful to Christ*

Introduction

I.   Commendation of the church in Pergamum, v. 13

    A. Christ knew about the hostile environment in Pergamum, v. 13a

    B. Christ commended the faithfulness of the church in Pergamum, v. 13b

II. Condemnation of some members of the church in Pergamum, vv. 14–15

    A. Those who followed the false teaching of Balaam were condemned, v. 14

    B. Those who practised the false teaching of Nicolas were condemned, v. 15

    C. Those who were condemned needed to repent, vv. 12, 16

III. The reward for those who overcome, v. 17

    A. Hidden manna

    B. A white stone

Conclusion

APPENDIX 2

EXAMPLES OF DIFFERENT STYLES OF SERMONS

The following three sample sermons provide practical examples of what we have discussed in this book. These are sermons I have prepared and preached over the years. I have revised and simplified them so that they can more easily be used as a teaching tool to demonstrate the principles of good sermon preparation and delivery, for those who wish to present the Scriptures in Africa in an organized way.

Readers are free to preach either all or some of these sample sermons if they consider them helpful. As a Christian and as an African, it is my duty and joy to share with others. Both the Bible (Phil 2:3–4; Matt 22:37–39) and my cultural heritage teach us to share things in common. It will be an added joy to me if these sermons are considered worthy to be preached to God's people for the honour of his name and to his glory.

However, it is also important to note that since the country I live in and the congregations to whom I preached these sermons are not exactly the same as yours, you may need to adapt the illustrations, definitions, explanations, questions, and applications to suit your context.

SERMON FROM THE LIFE OF KING JEHOSHAPHAT

Text: *2 Chronicles 20:1–30*
Topic: *The power of prayer and praise*
Purpose: *To encourage Christians not to give up in the face of dangers but rather to turn in faith to God for the solution*

Introduction

Do you know what it is to be afraid? When you were a child, were you afraid of people who bullied you? Are you afraid that someone at your workplace is trying to get you fired? Are you afraid of terrorism? Or a rebellion or a civil war? Or even a war between neighbouring countries? That was what King Jehoshaphat faced, and he too was afraid.

Jehoshaphat became king of Judah after the death of his father Asa, who had ruled for forty-one years. But his father had been ill in his old age, and so it is possible that Jehoshaphat had ruled alongside him for a few years. He was 35 years old when he came to the throne, and he ruled Judah for 25 years between 872 BC and 848 BC (2 Chr 16–17).

King Jehoshaphat was a godly king. He knew and loved the God of Israel, and served him with all his heart. His knowledge of God and his love for him helped him use the power of prayer and praise to win a victory when three powerful nations (Moab, Ammon and Seir) formed an alliance against him (vv. 21–23).

We can learn from the attitude of King Jehoshaphat. I pray that what we learn will give us the right perspective on our fears and lead us to worship God more.

I. What King Jehoshaphat Did When He Faced Danger, vv. 3–12

A. He prayed to God, vv. 3–12

Jehoshaphat was given alarming news (v. 2). Three powerful kings had formed an alliance against him and they had already gathered their large armies and were marching to attack him. Not surprisingly, he was afraid. This was a natural human reaction. He knew that Judah's small army was no match for the advancing troops. But he was the king, and he knew that he had to do something other than just run away!

What would you have done if you had been in his shoes? Would you have consulted a diviner or a spiritualist? Or sent for your generals? Or asked the ruler of a neighbouring country to come and fight on your side? Jehoshaphat could have done any of these things. But, though he was frightened, he did not set out to consult an oracle or a soothsayer, nor did he ask a medium for advice, or ask some powerful king or military advisors for support. Instead, he consulted the God of his forefathers, the God of Israel. He declared an immediate period of prayer and fasting for all the people of Judah (v. 3), and he and the people gathered in God's temple. He led them in an honest prayer, in which he admitted, "We are powerless against this mighty army that is about to attack us. We do not know what to do, but we are looking to you for help" (v. 12 NLT).

How many of us take prayer that seriously? It is often the last thing we do, rather than the first thing we do when we face problems. And yet, like Jehoshaphat, we face enemies who are much more powerful than we are. We face them in this world and in the spiritual realm, as Paul reminded us when he said that "our struggle is not against flesh and blood, but against the rulers, against the authorities, against the powers of this dark world and against the spiritual forces of evil in the heavenly realms" (Eph 6:12). We need to learn that all the various aspects of Christian ministry we engage in – singing, evangelism, discipleship, pastoring, counselling, teaching in adult and children's Sunday Schools, etc. – will never be powerful and effective in transforming people's lives and promoting spiritual growth unless we back them up with the power of prayer.

Let me give you an example of what this means in practice. A friend told me about the choir of a church he had attended while studying in Lagos, Nigeria. All the choir members would gather to pray thirty minutes before the service began. Five minutes before the service began, they would take their places and begin to sing to usher in worshippers. That choir knew the importance of prayer and praise, like Jehoshaphat did.

If all of us who are involved in any form of Christian service would take time to pray before serving, our service would have more impact on souls than is being witnessed today.

But Jehoshaphat's example not only tells us that we ought to pray, it also gives us some ideas about how we should pray.

B. He knew who he was praying to, v. 6

In his passionate prayer, Jehoshaphat reveals what he knows about God. First of all, he addresses God as Lord. You will see that in many of your Bibles this word is written in capital letters. That indicates that the word Jehoshaphat used was "Yahweh", the holy name for God that had been revealed to Moses at Sinai. It was the covenant name of God that he had told the people of Israel to use. That is why in v. 7 Jehoshaphat can also call him "our God" and address him as "the God of our ancestors". Yet he also acknowledges that God is not only the God of his forefathers, but also the God of creation. That is why God rules "over all the kingdoms of the nations" and has no equal. Jehoshaphat was convinced that the God of Israel was the one true God who holds all he has created together.

Jehoshaphat knew that the God of Israel, who is Creator-King, is all-powerful. He testified to this truth in his prayer, "Power and might are in your hand, and no one can withstand you" (v. 6).

As Christians, we too need to know the God we worship, and be in such a close relationship with him that we can call him "our God". Jesus taught his disciples to address him in prayer as "Our Father" (Matt 6:9–10). The more we know about his power and what he has done in the past, the more we will be able to trust him when danger threatens.

C. He reminded God about his promise, vv. 7–9

In his prayer King Jehoshaphat remembered what God had done for his people in the past. God had delivered Israel from Egypt, protected the Israelites through forty years of travelling in the wilderness, he won victories for Israel in the wars the nation had fought, and so on (v. 7).

Above all, King Jehoshaphat remembered God's promise of deliverance and his answers to the prayers of King Solomon. At the dedication of the temple in Jerusalem, King Solomon had prayed like this:

> When your people go to war against their enemies, wherever you send them, and when they pray to you toward this city you have chosen and the temple I have built for your Name, then hear from heaven their prayer and their plea, and uphold their cause . . . Now, my God, may your eyes be open and your ears attentive to the prayers offered in this place. (2 Chr 6:34–45, 40)

And God had answered Solomon's prayer, saying

> I have heard your prayer and have chosen this place for myself as a temple for sacrifices. When I shut up the heavens so that

there is no rain, or command locusts to devour the land or send a plague among my people, if my people, who are called by my name, will humble themselves and pray and seek my face and turn from their wicked ways, then will I hear from heaven and will forgive their sin and will heal their land. Now my eyes will be open and my ears attentive to the prayers offered in this place. (2 Chr 7:12–15)

King Jehoshaphat knew that God is faithful, righteous and just and that he keeps his promises. He also knew that nothing is ever too hard or difficult for God to do. God himself had stated that when he rebuked Sarah for laughing in disbelief at the idea that she, an old woman, could have a child. In response, God had quietly asked, "Is anything impossible for the LORD?" (Gen 18:14 NET). And the Angel Gabriel made the same point when Mary wondered how she, a virgin, could become pregnant. He told her, "with God nothing will be impossible" (Luke 1:37 NKJ), for "what is impossible for people is possible with God" (Luke 18:27 NLT).

That is something else we need to remember when we are afraid. And the more we know of God's word and of the promises he has given us in it, the more we can draw on that when we pray.

D. He listened to God's answer, vv. 14–21

King Jehoshaphat admitted that he and all the people of Judah were helpless in the face of the advancing enemies. He depended totally on the power of the God of Israel to deliver his people from them. He trusted that God, who had won victories for Israel in the past, would do so again. So he prayed, "We do not know what to do, but our eyes are upon you" (v. 12).

God's answer to this prayer did not come to the king directly, but was given to him through a Levite. It was a message of assurance and encouragement. The coming battle would not be Jehoshaphat's battle but God's battle. The king would not even have to fight; God would fight for them, and they would see him at work.

On receiving this assurance, Jehoshaphat and all the people did not question it. Instead, they bowed down and worshipped God, and the choir "stood up and praised the LORD, the God of Israel with a very loud voice" (v. 19). That choir was singing and rejoicing while the danger still threatened because they had heard and believed God's message.

The singing continued the next day, when Jehoshaphat charged the people saying, "Have faith in the Lᴏʀᴅ your God and you will be upheld; have faith in his prophets and you will be successful" (v. 20). He then organized a singing team from among the Levites and put them in the lead, with the army following behind. As the Levites led the army forward, they sang, "Give thanks to the Lᴏʀᴅ, for his love endures forever" (v. 21b).

Like Jehoshaphat and the people of Judah, we need to turn to God in prayer, and depend absolutely on God to bring to pass what he has promised to do for his people in his word. These promises include blessings in the present as well as in the future, but the greatest of all is the spiritual security we enjoy as the children of God. This means that even if God does not intervene in some miraculous way and allows us or a loved one to die from some illness, or in a road accident, or in an attack by Boko Haram or any other group, we can trust that death is not the end, but merely the gateway to life with him.

God is sovereign, and we cannot force him or manipulate him to make him do what we want. Yet he is also faithful. So we should sing songs that worship him for who he is and for what he has done. We should celebrate his person, power, greatness and faithfulness to his promises. Our songs should be meaningful and soul-inspiring, songs that lighten burdened hearts and encourage us in our faith and walk with Christ.

II. The Result of King Jehoshaphat's Faith, vv. 22–26

As Jehoshaphat and his army marched singing to the battlefield, God went ahead of them and fought the battle on their behalf. When they arrived at their enemies' camp, all they saw were corpses. God had spread confusion in the camp, and the soldiers of Ammon, Moab and Seir had ended up fighting and killing each other. There was nothing left for the Judean army to do except collect the plunder the enemy had left behind.

Not only was victory won for the people of Judah, but they were blessed with great riches. This is indeed an example of the truth that when we care about God's business, he will take care of ours. Jesus told his disciples not to occupy themselves with the worries of this world.

Instead, they were to first seek God's kingdom, and all other things would be added as a bonus (Matt 6:19–20, 24–34).

Conclusion

God moved in a dramatic and extraordinary way for Jehoshaphat and Judah. He had done so in the past when he delivered the descendants of Abraham from slavery in Egypt; he would do so in the future when his Son was crucified and resurrected. He can still do this today. We too can experience God's power, presence and blessings in our lives. If God's people who truly know him pray to him when troubled, remind him of his promises and of his person in challenging times, depend on him for victory when faced with temptations, and are consistently filled with the Holy Spirit, God can certainly move in dramatic and extraordinary ways as he did for Jehoshaphat and Judah.

> God still moves, God still moves;
> in the hearts of his people, God still moves.
> He does not sleep nor does he slumber;
> God still moves, God still moves.

But there is also one other lesson we can learn from the experience of King Jehoshaphat of Judah. He knew the power of prayer and praise and he used them effectively to the honour and glory of the name of God.

Praise is a powerful element in the Christian life. Therefore, when you are faced with danger, worship God in song. When you are burdened with problems, worship God in song. When you have a decision to make but are confused because you do not know which way to take, worship God in song. Even when you are discouraged, disappointed, depressed, and have lost hope for living, learn to worship God in song and see what he will do for you.

There is also a challenge here for gospel musicians – are you composing songs that highlight the person and power of God? Pastors, are you leading your people to praise and worship God as you preach? Do your people know the God they worship, the promises he has made, and his great acts in the past? It is your task to instruct them so that they too can join in the great chorus of praise, expressed in our words and our actions. And as we praise God with our words and actions, other people may be drawn to Christ.

TOPICAL SERMON ON WELFARE SUNDAY

Text: *2 Kings 4:1–7*
Topic: *Avoiding the mistakes of the past*
Purpose: *Sermon was preached on a welfare Sunday to encourage church members to care for widows and the aged*

Introduction

We all know that there are more widows than widowers in our society, and that they are often in very sad situations. Not only are they missing the companionship of their husbands, but they also face many other challenges. Sometimes their in-laws lay claim to all that the husband owned, including the marital home, because they insist that what belonged to their brother belongs to his family, and they deny the widow any place in that family. They do not care if she is left destitute and homeless. Other widows may keep their home, but still battle to provide food, clothing and education for their children. They also have to deal with manipulative men who look for opportunities to take advantage of them sexually. And they have to face this alone, because often their changed status leads to their being shunned by their former friends.

Sadly, widows can experience some of these things even when they are among God's people. I could tell you sad stories about that today, but let me begin by talking about the situation of a widow whom we meet in 2 King 4.

I. The Struggles of a Student, v. 1

This widow had been married to a man who was one of "the company of the prophets" (v. 1). In other words, her husband was a student in what might have been called a school for prophets. They were the Old Testament equivalent of a Bible college or seminary. The prophetic schools seem to have begun around the time of Samuel, and continued to flourish in the days of prophets like Elijah and Elisha (1 Sam 10:5, 11; 2 Kgs 2:3, 5; 4:38–41).

The widow described her husband as a godly man, who "revered the LORD". In fact, he was the sort of person you would expect to be blessed and to enjoy a long life. But although this is a gift God often gives to those who love and serve him, he does not guarantee it. Sometimes, for reasons we do not understand, he allows bad things to happen that we do not expect. That is what had happened to this man, his wife and their two children. They lost their husband and father. We do not know how he died. It may have been in an accident, or it may have been an illness. There was very little medicine in those days, and people often died of illnesses that could be cured today (providing, of course, we can get to a doctor or a hospital).

There is also one other thing we know about this man. He was poor – so poor that he had had to borrow money to support his family. This was not unusual, for few prophets were wealthy. In 2 Kings 6:1–7 we meet another member of the company of prophets who is so poor that he does not even own an axe. He had to borrow one, and it was a disaster when its head flew off and fell into the water.

Does this sound familiar at all? There are many students at Bible colleges and seminaries, and even many faithful pastors, who struggle financially. Their clothes are old, and they have to try to grow a few vegetables if they are to have enough to eat. If a medical emergency arises or school fees need to be paid, they may have to borrow money. They are often even poorer than the people they serve.

(I know that there are some people who cynically say, "if you want to get rich, plant a church". And there are indeed a few very wealthy pastors – not all of whom are true pastors. Some of them are more like the false shepherds described in Ezekiel 34, who ate the sheep rather than caring for them. But do not let those exceptions distract you from noticing the needs of those who serve humbly and faithfully.)

II. The Failure of a Community, v. 2

When this poor seminary student died, his wife found herself facing a pile of unpaid debts. She must have found herself wondering over and over again, "Why did God allow my husband to die and leave me in such a terrible situation?" We too may wonder why God would allow such a pious man to die in disgrace as a debtor. He knew that students in the school of the prophets received little or no financial support. Was God fair to him? We ask similar questions whenever someone enrolled in active service of God dies unexpectedly. In fact, there are books with titles like *Where Is God When It Hurts?* and *When God Doesn't Make Sense.* If I were to write my own book on this topic I might title it

Sometimes God Doesn't Make Sense.

The widow in Elisha's day found herself in an extremely stressful situation, for there was almost no way for a woman on her own to earn money in ancient Israel. Besides which, she had two boys to care for and feed – and no money to do it with. All that she had in the house was "a small jar of olive oil" (v. 2).

To make matters worse, the person to whom her dead husband owed the money lacked compassion. He showed no pity for the bereaved woman's suffering. This man was probably also an Israelite, one of the people of God, but he ignored passages in the law that said "Do not deprive the foreigner or the fatherless of justice, or take the cloak of the widow as a pledge" (Deut 24:17). In fact he ignored all that the law of Moses said about caring for strangers, orphans and widows. All he was interested in was getting his money back.

The part of the law that he did focus on was the part that allowed him to take the man's two sons as slaves in payment of the debt. This poor woman, the wife of a pastor, had lost her husband and now she was about to lose her children too! This was a disaster, not only because she loved them but also because as her sons grew they might eventually have been able to provide for her and help her grow some small food crop. Without any sons, she was doomed to extreme poverty, and might even be forced into prostitution to stay alive. But did the creditor care? Not a bit!

We are shocked at the creditor's attitude. How could he be so cruel? But wait a minute – let us look at ourselves too. If we have lent something to someone, do we demand it back, even when we know that paying us back will mean that the family cannot send their daughter to school? Do we place a higher value on money than on mercy?

"No!" you say. "I would never do that. Moreover, I am so poor that I don't have enough to lend anyone! So I could never be like this creditor." That may be true – you may never be the person who lends. But there is another side to this picture. Do you notice that it is the widow who has to go and talk to Elisha about her problems? And she seems to be on her own. Where were her husband's classmates? Why hadn't they approached the prophet on her behalf? They were acting like the people who stop being friends with someone when they are widowed. Is that not a terrible failure of love too?

And where were the man's relatives and the woman's family? Where were the rest of the community? There is no evidence that they had approached the creditor and asked to negotiate on her behalf. And when the creditor insisted on repayment, why had they not come together to rally round her and help her pay off the debt? The sum cannot have been huge (poor men are not lent large sums of money). Could they not have scraped together enough money to redeem at least one of the two sons, if not both of them? This was a godly couple, who must have been raised in a religious community, and yet the community turned its back on her when she was in need.

Sadly, that sometimes happens in our churches too. We are too busy with our own lives, too wrapped up in our own concerns, to see the need of others and work to meet it. In fact, we may even avoid people who are in trouble, afraid that they will ask us for help! If we do this, we cannot point fingers at the greedy creditors without recognizing that we ourselves are also guilty of a lack of compassion.

Even though we know that Paul told the Philippians, "Do nothing out of selfish ambition or vain conceit ... Each of you should look not only to your own interests, but also to the interests of others" (Phil 2:3–4), we too often fail to obey this instruction as individuals and as a Christian community.

"No," you say, "I do care for people who are in trouble". Do you? Does your whole church do that? What do you do when a seminary student dies in the unrest in Jos? If you know his or her family, do you check up on how they are doing? Not just in the week of the funeral, but in the months and years that follow?

And on this welfare Sunday, let me also remind you about another group for whom we need to show compassion. That is the elderly, those who have served us in the past but can no longer provide for their own needs.

This point was brought home to me very forcefully when I visited the Rev. Philip Gambo, the pastor who had dedicated our firstborn daughter, Dorcas Andih. He eventually retired from active pastoral ministry, and my wife and I visited him about two years prior to his death. We brought with us a few gifts and a small amount of money to help cushion the effects of his retirement. He thanked us profusely for our visit and for these gifts.

But we were shocked to discover two things. One was how poor he had become with only his wife's meagre income to live on. The other was that he told us that no one else had ever done what we had done for him and his wife since his retirement from service. And we had done so little!

As we drove back home, I kept asking myself, "Where are the churches that this man laboured for all his life? Where are the members that this man invested all his life into? Why do none of them remember the retired prophet?"

That a student of the prophetic school died with debt for lack of support for his ministry and that his two sons were at risk of being taken as payment for that debt signals a failure on the part of the community. That a retired minister was reduced to a life of poverty because neither the churches nor the people whom he invested his life in cared to support him in retirement is another failure. So is the fact that the denomination he served did not provide adequate retirement benefits to its pastors who had served long and faithfully.

Are we willing to allow such failures to continue? Or are we going to take steps to avoid them in future?

III. How to Avoid Repeating the Mistakes of the Past vv. 2–7

In the case of the widow in Israel, the prophet Elisha was at hand to salvage the situation so she could save her two sons (vv. 2–7). He performed a miracle that gave her the resources she needed to survive.

But God does not expect us to rely on miracles. He expects us to care for each other. This is abundantly clear from the instructions he gave about caring for the poor in the law of Moses. And those instructions are repeated in the New Testament, when Jesus commands us to love each other and to love our neighbours. In fact, in his letter James pours scorn on those who are happy to tell the poor that God will provide:

> Suppose a brother or a sister is without clothes and daily food. If one of you says to them, "Go in peace; keep warm and well fed," but does nothing about their physical needs, what good is it? In the same way, faith by itself, if it is not accompanied by action, is dead. (Jas 2:15–17)

We as individuals and as churches need to learn how to stand up for the rights of widows, to help them when their property is ripped away by greedy in-laws, to encourage them with our company, and to help them assemble the resources they need to be able to earn a living honestly – which is what Elisha did for the widow we have been talking about when he told her: "Go, sell the oil and pay your debts. You and your sons can live on what is left" (v. 7).

We also, as individuals and as churches, need to learn to care for those who have nurtured us in the past and are no longer able to do so. We do this by showing appreciation for what they did for us, visiting them and spending time with them, and by sharing what we have with them. Maybe the only thing you have to share is a meal – but there are many elderly people who would be very grateful for a chance to sit down with a family and share a good meal.

Those of you who are in business or in leadership – let me appeal to you to fix what was left undone in order not to repeat the ugly side of history. Pay your workers and your pastors an adequate salary, so that those who serve you faithfully are not burdened by worries about debt. If at all possible, set up some pension fund that will help to provide for their needs once they are unable to carry on working.

Conclusion

So here is my challenge to you this morning. What are you going to do about what you have heard? Some of the actions I have called you to are the work of months and years. You need to adjust your heart to see the needs of students, widows and the elderly and to be moved to compassionate action when you see a need you can help in any way.

But there is also one action that you can take right now, or in the course of this week: I want you to think about all the pastors you have known, and any students you know who are studying for the pastorate. Some of them may still be in this church, others may be away in seminary, others may have moved on to other pastorates. Some may have retired and others have died, leaving widows and children. Can I urge you to seek out one of those students or pastors and thank them for the work they are doing and have done in order to serve you and the rest of the congregation? Thank students for the time they are putting into learning how to serve God's church, thank pastors for the long hours they have spent teaching you, praying with you, encouraging you, comforting you, and preparing the sermons they preach to you. Your thanks alone will be a great encouragement to them, but it will be even better if you can take them some small gift, sharing your material and financial resources with those who have served you faithfully. As Paul says, "Anyone who receives instruction in the word must share all good things with his instructor" (Gal 6:6).

But do not let your kindness stop with your pastors. Keep your eyes open to make sure that there is no one among us who is in a situation of quiet desperation, like the widow whom Elisha helped. If you see such a person, rally round them and show them what Christian love means in practice.

EXPOSITORY SERMON ON LOOKING FOR THE GOOD

Topic: Can we get good food out of a broken clay pot?
Text: Philippians 1:12–18c
Purpose: To encourage Christians to see the good side of every bad experience

Introduction

A few of you here today may be old enough to remember the days when food was still cooked in clay pots. Today, we tend to use metal pots, but there was a time when clay pots and jars were common in every village. Water was stored in clay jars and so was grain. Beer was brewed and stored in clay pots and jars and food was cooked in clay pots. Everyone used them.

But the problem with a clay pot is that it breaks easily. Sometimes, when a woman was holding a pot full of freshly cooked food, something would happen and the pot would slip from her hand. When it hit the ground, it would crack or shatter. You would think that would mean that all the food would be wasted. But that was not what happened. There would still be some food in the cracked pot or clinging to the fragments of the pot. People knew that food could still be found in a broken clay pot, and so they would pick up the pieces and still find something to eat.

Now try thinking about your life as if it were a clay pot. There are days when that pot is beautiful and fulfilling its function well. Then we are happy and we rejoice and celebrate. But there are other days when we find ourselves wondering whether we are dropped pots. Things have been going well, and then all of a sudden something bad happens, and our good life is cracked and shattered. It is as if we have just watched the meal we were about to enjoy fall to the floor. We experience unhappiness, sadness, and pain. We find ourselves asking, "Why?", "Why me?" and "What have I done wrong?"

Christians also ask these questions because we are human beings living in the real world affected by sin. We feel that we are now useless, and that all our plans have gone wrong. What do we do on the days when we feel like that?

One thing I do when I have days like that is look at the experience of the Apostle Paul. He was someone who knew how to answer the question, "Can good food really come out of a broken clay pot?" He proves that by what he says in Philippians 1:12–18, the passage we read today.

I. Paul's Imprisonment Was for Good; It Advanced the Gospel, vv. 12–14

When Paul wrote his letter to the Philippians, he was in prison. Prison is not a good place to be. Prisons are dirty, dark, crowded. Some of the prisoners are dangerous. The guards are not interested in your problems. But even if you are in a relatively good prison, as Paul now was (he was under house arrest, not in the common jail – Acts 28:30) there is still the problem that you cannot go where you want or do what you want. You cannot leave the house. And Paul's letter tells us that he was in chains – unable to move freely. This must have been hard for Paul, who was an energetic man, always eager to set off on a new missionary journey to proclaim Christ, or eager to strengthen the new converts he had made. Prison was not a place he wanted to be. His plans had gone wrong, and he could have felt useless, unable to pursue the mission to Spain that he had been planning (Rom 15:28). He could have become very depressed. But look at what he wrote when he managed to send a letter out from his prison – Does he sound depressed to you?

No one who was deeply depressed would speak like this: "Now I want you to know, brothers and sisters, that what has happened to me has actually served to advance the gospel" (v. 12). He saw beyond his suffering and recognized that something positive was also happening.

What is he referring to when he speaks about "what has happened to me"? He may be referring to all the events described in Acts 21:17–28:31, which led to his ending up under house arrest in Rome. These events included a beating by a mob, imprisonment, an assassination attempt, years in jail and a terrifying storm that ended in a shipwreck. None of these were pleasant. And to make matters worse, there were people who disliked him and spread slanders about him. Even worse, some of those who did this were Christians who were envious of Paul's reputation and wanted to "stir up trouble" for him even though he was in prison. They were motivated by "envy, rivalry, and selfish ambition" (Phil 1:15–17).

The people who received his letter must have scratched their heads. They had heard what was going on. How could all of these very unpleasant things possibly serve to advance the gospel?

So Paul explains: His long journey and his imprisonment and the fact that others were saying bad things about him had made his jailers interested in him. What had he done to make so many people hate him? He did not look very dangerous! So they talked to him while they were guarding him, and they talked to each other about him. Some of them were probably even listening while he dictated this letter!

Not only that, but because his case was to be heard by Caesar himself (see Acts 25:11–12), his jailers were not common soldiers but were palace guards – people whom Paul would never have been able to preach to in ordinary circumstances. But now they, and anyone else who was interested, all knew that Paul was in prison ("in chains") not because he had done anything wrong but because of his religious belief in Christ (v. 13). This made them curious about his faith, and some of them may even have come to faith in Christ. He had found a mission field in prison! So that was one good result of his very bad situation.

But that wasn't the only good thing to come of it. Paul's behaviour had also been watched by the Christians in Rome. They admired his brave attitude in his unpleasant circumstances and they decided to follow his example of boldness and trust. So instead of Paul being the only preacher in Rome, there were now a lot of preachers, all "confident in the Lord" and daring to "proclaim the gospel without fear" (v. 14). So not only had his imprisonment given him a new mission field, it had also inspired many others to be missionaries!

No wonder Paul could happily assert that "what has happened to me has actually served to advance the gospel" (v. 12).

Paul's words remind us that God can make something good out of a bad human experience. God has the power to make good food come out of a broken clay pot. We need to remember this when bad things happened to us.

If Paul had settled into a life of despair, asking God "why" or "why me", or if he had given in to self-pity and misery, the soldiers who guarded him would have ignored him, and the outside world would have forgotten him. This would have crippled the spread of the gospel. But Paul found plenty of good food in the broken pot of his dreams, and that is why he could still rejoice, even though he was in chains.

What does this mean for us? Well, let me give you another example. There was a village pastor who planted maize in a year when drought hit the area. When he went to his field and saw how pale and discouraging the leaves looked, he looked up to heaven and sang a Hausa hymn, "Me za mu ce da Yesu?", which teaches that we cannot question God's actions. The next year, he again planted maize, and this time there was no drought. When he saw how green his crops were and how well they were growing, he sang another Hausa hymn, "Alhamdu ga Allah don Dansa Yesu" [Praise God for his Son Jesus]. He gave glory to God in every situation.

That village pastor knew the same truth that Paul did – God is in control whatever our circumstances, whether our situation is good or bad. But we tend to forget it. We want God's answer to our prayers to be always "Yes" and never "No". We forget Job's rebuke to his wife: "You are talking like a foolish woman. Shall we accept good from God, and not trouble?" (Job 2:9–10). What human beings see as "good" is not necessarily what God sees as good. Similarly, what we understand as "bad" is not bad to him. After all, how would a serious Christian know that he or she is growing spiritually if no negative experiences ever came their way?

As Lynda Randle sings,

The God on the mountain is still God in the valley.
The God of the day is still God in the night.

II. The Opposition to Paul Was for Good; It Made Christ Known, vv. 15–18c

There were Christians who did not like Paul. He mentions them in 1 Corinthians, where he speaks of "those who sit in judgement on me" (1 Cor 9:3). In 2 Corinthians, he sarcastically refers to these people as "super-apostles" (2 Cor 11:5), because they think they are so superior to him. These people were happy to know that Paul was in prison, and were all the more eager to preach in his absence. They are the people he is referring to when he says that "some preach Christ out of envy and rivalry".

Although he knew that their reasons for preaching were suspect and that they wanted to hurt him, Paul did not let that bother him. He knew that, whatever their motives for preaching, they were still preaching Christ and making him known. That was enough reason for Paul to rejoice, because the aim of his ministry was not to benefit himself but to make Christ known, and that was exactly what was happening.

III. There Are No Accidents with God

Paul's positive attitude to all that was happening would have taught the Philippian Christians an important truth. They learnt that there are no accidents with God. Instead of reducing the spread of the gospel, Paul's being in prison had expanded it wider than expected. The opposition to Paul and to his ministry had resulted in even more people in new places coming to know more about Christ. Like Joseph's brothers who inflicted so much pain on him, the people who opposed Paul had evil intentions but God used the situation for good (see Gen 50:20). Good food can still be gotten from a broken clay pot!

God can use every bad situation to bring glory to his name. So we have to trust him and remember Psalm 46:10: "Be still, and know that I am God; I will be exalted among the nations, I will be exalted in the earth."

Let me give you another example of God doing this in history. The great German Reformer Martin Luther is now celebrated as a hero by Protestant Christians. But when he started out, he was an obscure monk who was complaining about some doctrines and practices of the Roman Catholic Church. When he posted a list of his complaints on a church door, the pope was furious and ordered Luther to be arrested and put on trial. But the pope's action backfired. The incident that had occurred in a small town in Germany began to attract international attention. Instead of silencing Luther, the trial spread his message. God used Luther's difficult experience of being brought to trial for the good of his church. Just imagine what the story would be like today if Luther had begged for forgiveness when the pope had him arrested and had promised never again to mention the errors he had noticed in the church.

There may also be some of you in the church today who have seen how God has taken bad circumstances in which you found yourself and has used them to accomplish something good. If so, don't keep these stories to yourself. Share them with one another after this service so that we may all be encouraged.

But what about those of you who are still in difficult circumstances and don't yet see how God is going to turn them to good? For you, there are two things to learn:

First, you should not be surprised when bad things happen to you. Jesus warned his followers that they would not have an easy time because they are going against the spirit of the times. The truth will always be opposed because it exposes and confronts what is evil, and people do not like this. The prophet Micaiah was imprisoned by King Ahab because he dared to tell the king the truth (1 Kgs 22:1–28). Jesus himself was rejected, hated and crucified.

Second, we should refuse to let our circumstances get on top of us. Rather than looking only at the bad side of what is happening, we should trust in God and look for ways in which God can be glorified through what is happening to us. We too should look for the good food in the broken pot.

When we as Christians seek to interpret all the bad things that happen to us as God would interpret them, our eyes will be opened to understand what God is doing in history. God expects his children to depend on him in all situations. Jesus told his first disciples to depend on him as they would not be able to do anything apart from him (John 15:5). Paul was aware of this truth. Therefore, he drew his strength, power, confidence and boldness for preaching the gospel from Jesus

Christ. When trouble came, he did not become stressed but committed himself into God's hand, and continued to preach the gospel of Jesus Christ and praise God in his new circumstances.

Conclusion

This old hymn sums up what we need to know when times are dark:

> There's not an hour that He is not near us,
> No, not one! No, not one!
> No night so dark but His love can cheer us,
> No, not one! No, not one!
>
> Jesus knows all about our struggles,
> He will guide till the day is done;
> There's not a friend like the lowly Jesus,
> No, not one! No not one!

www.ingramcontent.com/pod-product-compliance
Lightning Source LLC
Chambersburg PA
CBHW071826090426
42737CB00012B/2190